BUILDING A HOUSE IN NEW FRANCE

An Account of the Perplexities of Client and Craftsmen in Early Canada

LE MASSON

The pretty wife of a coarse stone mason delivering a meal to the work site.

"By Heaven, this oaf of a mason has a wife who is too beautiful,
I would gladly take up the trowel to be able to enjoy such a young lass,
By his uncouth appearance I would guess that while he builds for others,
At his house and on the sly others often work in his place."

PETER N. MOOGK

BUILDING A HOUSE IN NEW FRANCE

**An Account of the Perplexities of Client
and Craftsmen in Early Canada**

**Winner of the Sainte-Marie Prize in History, 1975
Historical Sites Branch
Ontario Ministry of Natural Resources**

McClelland and Stewart

This book is dedicated to the memory of my grand-father, Hugh R. Shuttleworth, and of his brother, "Uncle Ed," whose memories of Ontario before the First World War gave me a sense of my own roots in Canada's past.

The Canadian Publishers
McClelland and Stewart Limited
25 Hollinger Road
Toronto, Ontario

Printed and bound in Canada

Contents

Preface - W.J. Eccles/7
Foreword/8
Introduction/11
1. The Legal Maze/13
2. The *Canadien* Farmhouse/22
3. From Wood to Stone/49
4. A Tale of Two Houses/73
5. The Merchant Builders/88
6. "If it falls down, it will have to be mended"/110
Conclusion/119
Appendix A: Glossary of French Terms/122
Appendix B: Principal Contract for the
Jean-Baptiste Forestier House/125
Bibliography/130
Credits/137
Index/139

Jurors' Statement

As jurors, we have unanimously selected the manuscript, "Building a House in New France", as winner of the 1975 Sainte Marie Prize, for the impressive amount of research and scholarly contribution to the knowledge and understanding of seventeenth century Canada

John Moir
University of
Toronto

Bruce Trigger
McGill University
Montreal

Marcel Trudel
University of
Ottawa

Preface

The idea for this book was born in a seminar on the history of Canadian architecture conducted at the University of Toronto by the late Bill Goulding. It seemed odd that we knew so little about the people who had built those historic structures whose physical characteristics were thoroughly studied. It was from that point that I began my exploration into the social background of housebuilding in New France. That was in the spring of 1969 and it was only in the autumn of 1975, while on sabbatical with a Canada Council fellowship, that I had time enough to sort out the accumulated information and to put an account into writing. The Sainte-Marie Prize in Canadian History provided the incentive and a deadline, without which many things would not be completed.

Though this book considers the human dimension of house construction, it contains information on the techniques of building during the French regime. It is hard to explain one without dealing with the other and some of the remarks on structure are based on casual observations made while walking about the old sections of Montreal and Quebec City. The information on the builders and their clients was gleaned by more extended labours in the notarial and judicial archives. It is hoped that the reader will not find the text too "dry" and that this book will be a new and agreeable road for visiting French Canada as it was before 1760.

There are two people whose help and advice has been particularly useful in aiding my research. A.J.H. "Jack" Richardson of the Historic Sites Branch of Canada's Department of Indian Affairs and Northern Resources is well known as an encyclopedia of building data. In addition to the material he has given to me over the years, he also provided an opportunity for collecting further information by engaging me to do research on the builder-contractors of New France for the department. One of the pleasures of being a visiting historian at the Fortress of Louisbourg in 1975-76 has been to work with Eric R. Krause, an historian who is the arbiter of authenticity in French regime construction. Eric has kept me from falling into too many holes of my own making. A word of thanks is also due to George C. Ingram, a fellow graduate student at Toronto, who drew my attention to *pièces-sur-pièces* construction. It should also be said that my wife Susan and my two sons, Jonathan and Benjamin, endured much as I fought losing battles with the typewriter.

Peter N. Moogk

Foreword

It has been estimated that the total number of emigrants from France to Canada before the Conquest was some ten thousand, the vast majority of them arriving in the second half of the seventeenth century. Once here they found themselves in a hostile environment, having a climate far more extreme than anything they could have experienced in France. Shelter from the elements assumed an even greater importance in Canada than it had had for them in Europe. Without adequate housing there could be little hope of survival. This work by Professor Moogk on how houses were built in New France is, therefore, of prime importance in our search to understand what life was really like for those early settlers, and that, after all, is what the study of history is all about.

When these settlers came from France in the seventeenth century they brought with them their social, political, and religious institutions. They constituted a small segment of French society transported across the Atlantic to the North American wilderness. Inevitably, however, they had to adapt many of their old ways of doing things to their new environment.

A main strength of Professor Moogk's study is the careful manner in which he traces the way the settlers modified their house construction techniques. In the early days they built their homes in the same fashion as had their medieval ancestors in northwestern France, where timber was scarce. Beginning with a wooden frame and upright studs, the spaces between were filled with stone rubble and mortar, known as *colombage*. The steep pitch of the roof required to shed heavy rainfall off thatch was retained in Canada. A generation later, faced with a limitless supply of timber, the Canadians began to use squared timber laid horizontally between the posts instead of stone rubble. The result was a solid structure, easily constructed, and possessed of excellent insulation qualities against the cruel winter cold.

In the eighteenth century, with the struggle for mere survival won, and a degree of affluence unknown among the peasants of France beginning to spread through the colony, the Canadians began to build the well proportioned solid masonry homes that delight the eye to this day. A more graceful architectural style has yet to be produced in this country.

The elucidation of this development, the detailed study of exactly how these homes were built, required long hours of patient research in the *greffes* of the seventeenth and eighteenth century notaries. Hundreds of contracts had to be analysed. Beyond that, historical imagination and literary skill were required to transform that raw material into a meaningful narrative account. Professor Moogk has acquitted himself well in this arduous task. He has succeeded in producing a work that will be of great value to other toilers in the vineyard, and to students of history at large. His book is certainly worthy of the Sainte-Marie Prize and he is to be congratulated on its having been bestowed on him. The Government of Ontario is to be commended on its having had the wit to establish the prize as part of its historic site programme at Sainte-Marie to stimulate interest in the heritage of our past.

W.J. Eccles
Professor of History
University of Toronto

Introduction

Much has been written about the architecture of completed buildings, but very little has been said about the process that brought them into being. A house can be seen as the culmination of an event that is as fascinating as the product itself. In the case of New France, or Canada under the French Crown, this neglect cannot be explained by an inadequacy of the historical sources. The truth is that no other craft activity was as well documented as was the construction of buildings. There are thousands of building contracts made between 1640 and 1760 that are available to the modern researcher. In most cases they were agreements made before notaries and these deeds have survived because the notarial files were deposited with the local court after the notary's death. The contracts involved carpenters, masons, general contractors, joiners, roofers, metalworkers and labourers and they record each stage in the building of private houses in the French colony. A few hundred were selected from various periods of the colony's history to obtain a general picture of the practices and problems of the builders. Court records and travellers' letters helped to complete the picture. The sample of French deeds consulted was too small to allow one to say anything significant, except that there was a precedent in seventeenth century France for most Canadian building procedures. Statements on the building usages of the mother country rely largely on a number of architectural handbooks available to the contemporary builder.

One could as easily reconstruct the history of church buildings and of government structures, and this has been done in a few cases.[1] These buildings, however, do not express popular values as well as does the private dwelling. The construction of institutional buildings was more uniform and impersonal and their design was strongly influenced at all times by the fashions of the mother country. When, for example, the

Crown wished to erect fortifications, the specifications and plans were drawn up by a King's Engineer, who referred to handbooks of military architecture for guidance. The building contract was then put out for bidding by private masonry contractors. It was a standard procedure that tells us little about life in the colony. In the rural parishes when the church-wardens (with clerical prodding) decided to build a church or rectory, an assembly was called by the intendant. In the presence of the priest, militia captain and seigneur, the parishioners selected *syndics* to levy contri-butions of labour and of materials and to oversee the work. This event lacked the spontaneity of a building "bee" in the English-speaking colo-nies of North America and the process was drawn out as each family's contribution was extracted or grudgingly given by the countryfolk.

Since the *Canadiens*, by all accounts, were notably wilful and indepen-dent, it is appropriate that we study the history of the domestic house in New France, since the home was expressive of the individual. It also re-flected the nature of the *Canadiens*. Through the various types of construc-tion and building procedures, it is possible to trace the cultural evolution of French Canada and to measure the growth in private fortunes. This is not to say that the individual home was the unrestrained expression of wealth and of personal taste. It is axiomatic that the builder must consider the climate and accomodate himself to the natural resources at hand. The process of constructing a private house followed a freer pattern than insti-tutional construction, but in both cases the builder's freedom was tem-pered by natural factors and by the law. In New France the effect of the law was most visible in the towns and so, this is where our story will begin.

NOTES

1. Wilfrid and Elsie McLeod Jury, *Sainte-Marie Among the Hurons* (Toronto, 1954); Pierre-Georges Roy, "Notes et documents sur le Palais de L'Intend-ance, à Québec," *Bulletin des Recherches historiques* [hereafter B.R.H.], Vol. XXXV (1929), 597-611, 651-670; Ramsay Traquair, *The Old Architecture of Quebec* (Toronto, 1947), in which Professor Traquair reconstructs the history of several ecclesiastical buildings.

1

The Legal Maze

The administrators in New France had a passion for visible order and symmetry. In all of the major towns an attempt was made to plan their growth and to enforce official road allowances. The first known town plan was that of Governor Huault de Montmagny for the "city" of Quebec in 1636.[1] Though this settlement at the narrows on the St. Lawrence River had been permanently established in 1608, the European population of the entire colony did not exceed 250 souls in 1636. Quebec was still a small French outpost serving as a base for the fur trade and for the Christian missionaries to the Amerindians. The progress of New France was lethargic and the colony's ability to survive was in doubt until 1663 when Louis XIV assumed direct rule of Canada from the trading companies that had administered the colony in the king's name. Official encouragement to immigration in the 1660s raised the white population to about 6,500 persons in 1672 and then France's wars against Germany and the Netherlands diverted the monarch's money and interest away from the colony.

By 1672 confidence in Canada's future led to the first effective measures in town planning. In that year François Dollier de Casson, superior of the Sulpician Fathers who were the lords of Montreal Island, marked out the streets of "Ville Marie de Montréal." This westernmost settlement in the St. Lawrence valley had been founded 30 years before and was harassed by the Iroquois Confederacy that looked upon the community as an intrusion into its territory. In 1672 as well Governor-General Buade de Frontenac gave the case for regulating Quebec's development. "Nothing," he wrote to the Minister of the Navy and Colonies, "has appeared to me to be so fine and so magnificent as the location of the town of Quebec [. . .], but I find, or rather it seems to me, that a very grave error has been committed in allowing private individuals to build houses according to their own

13

fancy and without any order [. . .]. I believe that one should consider not only the present situation, but also the future state of things." He proposed that the minister endorse a plan for the fortification of the town "and to mark thereon the streets and squares that would be established, so that subsequently, when some individual wishes to build, he will do so with symmetry and in a manner that might contribute to the beautification and the embellishment of the town."[2] Frontenac did not await a reply; in March 1673 he forbade further construction unless authorized by himself and in conformity with the projected street alignments "to give, by this means, some form and symmetry to a town that one day must be the capital of an immense country."[3] Earlier, in 1665, the current governor and the *Conseil souverain* had acted to maintain the width of an existing street;[4] Frontenac proposed that these street allowances be laid down well in advance of construction.

The Lower Town of Quebec was too well advanced in its haphazard growth and its site was too confined to yield to a vision of broad avenues and expansive squares. In the 1680s, however, the small Place Royale was created with the monarch's bust in bronze as its centrepiece and a minimum width of twelve *pieds* was set for the Lower Town's streets.[5] The same road allowance was chosen for Trois-Rivières in 1735, nearly a century after that town had been established.[6] The Upper Town of Quebec was still malleable in the seventeenth century and two arteries, Saint-Jean and Saint-Louis streets, were run parallel to one another through the town. One began at the "grand place" before the cathedral and the other led from the governor's fort to the main road that, by 1734, linked the towns in the St. Lawrence valley. Montreal had the advantage of a more open and level location. In 1721 that town excited the admiration of Father Charlevoix: "It is well situated, well built and with ready access to the river [. . .] Montreal is a long rectangle."[7] After the irregularity of Quebec and Trois-Rivières, Montreal appeared orderly and regular, even if the streets within the town were not really parallel. A rectilinear grid was the ideal and this is the form given to the extensions of Quebec in the wishful plans of government engineers. None of the towns along the St. Lawrence River ever fulfilled the dream.

Louisbourg on Cape Breton Island came closest to the ideal because the planners acted during the infancy of the town and the Crown, as the principal landowner, gave out grants that conformed to the plan. By the Treaty of Utrecht in 1713 France surrendered Newfoundland and peninsular Acadia, and a new base had to be created for the ships engaged in the North American cod fishery, for the protection of the mouth of the St. Lawrence, and for the resettlement of the subjects from the ceded areas.

Cape Breton was chosen as the site for that new base. The first town plan for Louisbourg was prepared in 1717 and a definitive plan was approved in 1721 and published two years later.[8] Some misaligned buildings on government land were demolished and then, in dealing with established landowners, the administrators compromised. The two oldest streets, on the Presqu'Ile du Quay, were left as eccentrics and the decision to reserve the quayside for fisherman foundered on the resistance of the merchants and tavernkeepers already located there. As the principal economic support of Ile-Royale (Cape Breton), the cod fishery was given special consideration in the building laws of Louisbourg. An ordinance passed in 1721, but not enforced, limited houses to one full storey and a room height of seven *pieds* so that the breezes needed to dry the cod fillets would be unimpeded.[9] A contemporary law that required a clear area of 350 *toises* outside the town walls also made an exception for fishermen's huts and drying platforms.[10] At Montreal the defences were to have a clear line of fire for 500 *pieds* and, notwithstanding, Montrealers build houses on top of the fortifications and in front of them.[11] In 1688 the intendant had accused those who built houses outside the town walls of doing so "to have greater liberty to serve drinks, whether on forbidden days or at late hours, without fear of being caught by the police."[12] Outside all of the colony's towns the story was the same: suburbs with substantial homes grew up and the buildings had to be demolished when an attack was expected.

The royal administration wanted the towns of New France to be compact as well as defensible and these suburbs developed while there was still vacant land within the town walls. It was an absurd situation created, in part, by people who accumulated town lots for speculation. The intendants of the colony, whose jurisdiction extended to public order in the towns, tried to force the owners of unoccupied lots to either build on that land or to sell it to someone who would erect a house. In April, 1685, those with vacant land in Quebec's Lower Town were ordered to do just that by the following summer.[13] The law was ineffective, for it had to be reissued in 1707 with a provision for reuniting the empty lots to the royal domain.[14] It is remarkable that there was still unused land in an area whose confined location forced residents to build on small lots. At Montreal the demands of the intendant were modest; in 1688 each resident was restricted to owning one square *arpent* within the town and on that site the owner was to build "a house of stone and mortar or of heavy timber with a masonry chimney" within a year.[15] At Louisbourg the Crown, as grantor, could keep the size of town lots down to a quarter square *arpent* or less. Recipients of grants were enjoined in 1720 to build "the houses and storehouses along the street fronts" within a year of the concession or risk forfeiture of the land.[16] This policy seems draconian and yet, when one looks at town maps of the eighteenth century, it is apparent that the authorities tolerated the existence of large sections of vacant ground. The fact that many of the landowners concerned were religious orders may have held back decisive action.

In the countryside the situation was reversed. Intendant Jean Talon's effort in the 1670s to draw the rural folk into compact villages was against the general trend among the settlers to form straggling settlements of loosely-spaced houses. The desire for arable land fronting on the St. Lawrence River led to a subdivision of farms on the oldest *seigneuries* during the eighteenth century. It was against the public interest to allow farms to be reduced to thin strips that would be difficult to farm and inadequate for the support of a family. To avert this situation a royal ordinance issued in April, 1745, forbade the building of a house in the country, where no village had been established, on a lot that was less than one-and-a-half *arpents* wide and 30 to 40 *arpents* long.[17] This ordinance was enforced with surprising zeal by Intendant François Bigot who ordered the demolition of a number of houses built in contravention of the king's law.[18]

The royal officials in Canada evidently shared the creed of a contemporary French magistrate who declared that "the beauty of towns is principally derived from the alignment of their streets."[19] More attention was given to upholding street allowances than to the regulation of vacant town lots. Laws for the maintenance of thoroughfares in the towns were passed in 1673, 1685, 1686, 1689, 1727, 1732 and 1735. Under these laws builders were forbidden to begin construction without first having obtained an official alignment for the building. This was an established practice in the city of Paris, whose civil laws were a model for the colonies. In the town of Quebec the Overseer of Highways (*Grand Voyer*) and his deputies made the surveys and issued the alignments along the public thoroughfares. At Montreal, before the suppression of the seigneurial jurisdiction in 1693, this responsibility belonged to the *bailli*. To judge from the court records and the streets of the town, he neglected this duty. Prosecutions for encroachment on the roadways are hard to find and though the street allowances for Montreal were set at thirty *pieds* in 1688,[20] the actual width of the streets varied from eighteen to twenty-four *pieds*. The duty of the magistrates to maintain the right of way in the towns of New France was extended in 1686 to supervision of anything that might project into the street, such as steps, porches, shutters, signs, balconies and eaves.[21] Elevated, covered walks (*galeries*) were disliked by the authorities and they were outlawed, by implication, in 1727. The crown attorney at Quebec described one as a public hazard because the occupants of the house used it to throw "rubbish and other unseemly things" on the street below.[22]

House alignments were certainly enforced at Quebec, but not with consistency. Action was often taken when the offending structure was well underway or completed. There seems to have been no surveillance of builders as they began construction. Two months after the *Conseil souverain* had decreed, "It is forbidden [...] to build any house whose alignment has not been granted beforehand" a mason was ordered by the *Grand Voyer* to level the front wall of a misaligned, newly-built house. The mason's defence before the *Prévôté* was that he had never received any official delimitation of the property, though, presumably, he had asked for one.[23]

Quite apart from satisfying the demands of the authorities, a prospective builder and his client had to contend with neighbours. Louis Savot forewarned his readers to select a building site "removed from the dwellings of craftsmen whose trades entail great noise [...]" and to take care not to be "too close to churches for fear of being deafened by their bells nor too far away from them because of the inconvenience of reaching a church; if one is near to kin and close friends, to water, the market, work places" and one's home is located on a wide street, then all would be well.[24] Louis Liger, who rewrote Charles Estienne's enormously-popular book *La Maison Rustique*, advised readers bent on constructing a house to consider "first, whether the kitchen has a good foundation; secondly, if the land is truly his; whether there is not some minor, some heir, some creditor or some lord who might disturb him." In French civil law the inherited or acquired right to a landed property was sacrosanct, and it was not extinguished by sufferance or the passage of time as it might be under English Common Law. A thorough examination of one's title was advisable to make sure that no one else had an unexercised claim to that land. The physical limits of one's property also required verification. "I would even advise the buyer," wrote Liger, "to have all of his property surveyed and delimited in co-operation with his neighbours before building, so that even the most peevish ones will have nothing to complain about."[25] It was really in the towns of New France, where residents built on or close to the property line, that such precautions were essential. Residents of Louisbourg were obliged to maintain posts delimiting their property to put an end to "the court cases that arise all too often in the colonies over the limits of the said landholdings."[26] It was a false economy to dispense with these precautions, for a wall that encroached on a neighbour's land would lead to an order for its demolition or, at the very least, payment of substantial damages to the neighbour.[27]

Neighbours could be a help as well as a hazard to our townsman in New

France. Urban houses were usually aligned along the length of a street with their facades marking the limits of the roadway. Not only was it common to front on the street, but one customarily had one gable at the dividing line between properties. It was an excellent opportunity to use the gable as a common wall for two houses and thereby save each owner some money. Even if the neighbour were already well-housed, he might consent to share the costs of a common gable with an eye to future construction. In this case the builder would leave projecting stones (*pierres d'attente*) on the neighbour's side of the gable to support the lateral walls built at a later date.

From a few notarized agreements for a shared gable wall or *pignon mitoyen*, it appears that the simplest procedure was to have each party concede an equal amount of land for the wall and to divide the building costs in the same manner. If one party provided all of the land – a gable could be four *pieds* thick – he might be excused from contributing to the cost of construction. Mutual consent was required for the number and location of hearths, chimneys and cupboard recesses to be build into the gable.[28] In an accord made at Quebec in 1728 Joseph Hains, a joiner, conceded the land and Charles Hubert, *bourgeois*, agreed to bear the construction cost save for the chimney flue dividers (*languettes*). These would be paid for by Hains, who was also to supply a horse and cart "to excavate and carry away the earth and debris" as the foundations were dug and the gable built; the carter would be paid by Hubert.[29] Hains had consented to pay for the *languettes* by the cubic *toise* of masonry, as was then the custom when building chimneys, but when another mason appraised their value at 16 *livres* currency a *toise* the contractor went to court to demand more. He was forced to accept the appraised value of his work, especially since Hains refused to pay more and had himself filled the scaffolding holes in the gable and had set the arch (*clef*) in one fireplace.[30]

Once acquired, a common wall was maintained and repaired at joint expense. This was obligatory and a co-owner could legally compel the other to contribute to the rebuilding of the wall. Faced with such a demand, a resident of Quebec pleaded in 1748 that the erection of the new *mur mitoyen* be put off "since he can only find workers by paying excessive wages and, moreover, the wall cannot be built because all the masonry workers are required for either the fortifications or for wharves." This plea was rejected by the *Prévôté*.[31]

The *Coûtume de Paris*, the civil law used in New France, did not take good neighbourliness for granted. Of the 362 articles of the civil code, 17 dealt with the problems of the *mur mitoyen*. Their object was to protect property owners from inconveniences caused by the occupant of an adjo-

Even the barring of a window could be done with artistry.

ining property. A common or shared wall was not to be altered, pierced or encumbered by one party with impunity. The *Coûtume* prescribed the addition of protective walls (*contre-murs*) of a stated thickness and depth when a stable, forge, oven or latrine was located against or near the common wall.[32] This would protect the neighbouring household from the seepage of pollutants or the transmission of intense heat through the wall. One can doubt the efficacy of article 191 that required a four *pieds* wall of no specified depth between a well and a privy abuting the shared wall. The *Coûtume* was more effective in preserving property rights than in assuring sanitation. These rights included protection of one's privacy from the roving eye of the person next door. Under article 200, windows in a privately-owned wall fronting the adjacent property had to be nine *pieds* above ground level "fully glazed and with iron bars."[33] The nuns of the Montreal *Hôtel-Dieu* succeeded in compelling a private householder to seal up the second floor windows and dormers that overlooked their property.[34] Unlike many ordinances, the principles of the *Coûtume de Paris* were common knowledge among the populace and they were explicitly cited by litigants in building disputes.[35]

It is tempting to follow the development of building laws in the towns, but the town house is not representative of homes in New France. Moreover, the history of building legislation leads into the eighteenth century before we have considered the state of domestic housing in the earlier period. To "begin at the beginning," we should look at the construction of dwellings in seventeenth century Canada and, in particular, rural houses. Then, when we come to the urban house of the eighteenth century, we will be aware of the changes that have occurred in the pattern of construction.

NOTES

1. R.G. Thwaites (ed.), *The Jesuit Relations and Allied Documents.* 73 vols. (Cleveland, 1896-1901), IX, 137.
2. *Rapport de l'Archiviste de la Province de Québec* [hereafter R.A.P.Q.], 1926-1927, 11-12.
3. Pierre-Georges Roy (ed.), *Ordonnances, Commissions, etc., etc., des Gouverneurs et Intendants de la Nouvelle-France, 1639-1706* [hereafter O.C.G.I.]. 2 vols. (Beauceville, 1924), I, 135.
4. *Jugements de Délibérations du Conseil souverain de la Nouvelle-France* [hereafter J.D.C.S.]. 6 vols. (Quebec, 1885-91), I, 336-7.
5. O.C.G.I., II, 95.
6. Public Archives of Canada [hereafter P.A.C.], C11A series transcript, LXIV, 110-4.
7. Pierre François-Xavier de Charlevoix, *Histoire et Description Generale de la Nouvelle France.* 6 vols. (Paris, 1744), V, 202.
8. Archives Nationales de France, Archives de Colonies [hereafter A.N.,A.C.], série C11C, XVI, 31 mai 1723.
9. A.N., A.C., série B, XLIV, ff. 565vo-566.
10. *Ibid.*, ff. 546-547.
11. Pierre-Georges Roy, *Inventaire des ordonnances des intendants de la Nouvelle- France conservées aux archives provinciales de Québec* [hereafter I.O.I.]. 4 vols. (Beauceville, 1919), I, 141; O.C.G.I., II, 181-2.
12. O.C.G.I., II, 176.
13. O.C.G.I., II, 93-6.
14. I.O.I., I, 28.
15. O.C.G.I., II, 176.
16 A.N., A.C., série C11C, XV, ff.230-231.
17. *Edits, ordonnances royaux, déclarations et arrêts du Conseil d'Etat du Roi concernant le Canada* [hereafter E.O.R.]. 3 vols. (Quebec, 1854-56), II, 594-5; Pierre-Georges Roy, *Inventaire des jugements et délibérations du Conseil supérieur de la Nouvelle-France de 1717 à 1760* [hereafter I.J.D.C.S.]. 7 vols. (Beauceville, 1932-35), IV, 299.
18. E.O.R., II, 400, 594-5; I.O.I., III, 198.
19. Edmé de Freminville, *Dictionnaire ou traité de la police générale des villes* (Paris, 1758), 518.

20. O.C.G.I., II, 176.
21. J.D.C.S., I, 336-7; for an order to demolish an objectionable *saillie* in 1729, upon the complaint of the neighbours, see I.J.D.C.S., II, 70.
22. Archives du Québec [hereafter A.Q.], N.F. 19, IX (1676), ff. 12vo-13.
23. P.A.C., M.G. 8, B1 (Prévôté du Québec), III (1689), 213, 225-6.
24. Louis Savot (F. Blondel, ed.), *L'Architecture Françoise de Bastimens Particuliers* (Paris, 1685), 14. The advantage of a wide street was that it allowed greater sunlight to reach the windows and it permitted direct access by carriage to the house.
25. Louis Liger, *La Nouvelle Maison Rustique, ou Economie Generale de Tous les Biens de Campagne.* 2 vols. (Paris, 1755), I, 6. This work goes back to Charles Estienne's *Praedium Rusticum*, which was first published in 1554. Jean Liébault translated the work and republished it ten years later as *Agriculture et Maison Rustique*. Louis Liger was one of those who rewrote this French classic on rural life.
26. A.N., A.C., série B, XLIV, f.549vo (18 mars 1721).
27. I.J.D.C.S., I, 295; II, 70.
28. A.Q., Greffes des notaires du régime français [hereafter G.N.R.F.], J.E. Dubreuil, 17 mai 1724, 24 juin 1728; J. Pinguet, 16 mars 1728.
29. A.Q., G.N.R.F., J.E. Dubreuil, 27 avril 1728.
30. P.A.C., M.G. 8, B1, XX-3, 757-8, 852-6.
31. *Ibid.*, XXXVI, 80-3
32. Pierre Bullet, *Architecture Pratique* (Paris, 1780), 479-83; Pierre Lemaistre, *La Coûtume de la Prevosté et Vicomté de Paris* (Paris, 1700), 555-9. The *Coûtume*, in its definitive form of 1580, is the single body of French law bearing on construction that was regularly cited in Canadian courts. The magistrates may have been guided by French building ordinances, such as the *ordonnance générale* of Charles IX in 1560, whose article 96 dealt with obstructive projections, but this is not explicitly stated. Colonial building laws are, however, cited by name.
33. Pierre Bullet, 491.
34. A.N., A.C., série Moreau de Saint-Méry, II, f.70; I.J.D.C.S., I, 199, 227.
35. See, for example, two cases heard by the Quebec *Prévôté* in July 1707 in P.A.C., M.G. 8, B1, IX, 267-8, 313-5, 326-8. One involved the chimney of an armourer's *fourneau* built against a common wall and the other concerned a window in a stable overlooking the neighbouring property. Articles 199, 200 and 203 of the *Coûtume de Paris* were referred to in these cases.

2

The *Canadien* Farmhouse

In France there is not an exact prototype, in form *and* materials, for the *Canadien* farmhouse. It has been said that the oblong, hipped roof structures around Quebec City originated in Normandy and that the square homes with massive gables in the Montreal region can be traced to Brittany.[1] A parallel in styles exists, but it is not limited to those or adjoining provinces. Climate rather than regional tradition seems to have been the determinant in the selection of roof forms. The profile of the Quebec region house of the seventeenth and early eighteenth centuries, with its steep, hipped roof and bellcast eaves can be found in buildings in the hilly areas of southwestern France and the Massif Central as well as in the northern provinces of Normandy and Picardy.

The relationship of this form to climate was evident as I travelled in 1969 from La Rochelle to see the prehistoric cave drawings at Les Eyzies de Tayac. In the provinces of Aunis and Saintonge, the home of a fifth of the immigrants who had settled in New France, one could see no similarity between the long, low-lying white farmhouses with their tile roofs and the French-Canadian cottage. As one progressed upward through the valleys of the Isle and the Dordogne, the silhouette of the houses began to resemble that of the old homes in the Quebec area. The climate was also colder and more damp than it had been on the plains of Saintonge. Confirmation of the relationship of climate and roof structure came from Louis Savot's *L'Architecture Françoise*, a book that was written in the 1630s when the farms of the first French colonists were being cleared around Quebec. Savot observed that a steep roof which readily shed rain and snow, was desirable in "cold regions" because "if it were too low, the snow would accumulate on it and when it melted, it would form ridges of ice on the eaves; these ridges would cause the water to back up and to leak

The Villeneuve House at Charlesbourg, with its steep hipped roof, many windows and attenuated proportions, imitated buildings in the cold regions of seventeenth century France.

into the garret or attic.''[2] It appears that the roof of the *Canadien* farmhouse during the French regime, with a slope of around 55 degrees from the horizontal and whose height accounted for nearly two-thirds of the building's elevation, was a seventeenth century response to the climate of the St. Lawrence valley. The same form was likewise employed in the cold and rainy areas of contemporary France.

The colonists of New France reproduced French forms in new materials. There was no analogy between the timber houses with board or shingle roofs built in Canada and homes in France, except for farm outbuildings, mountain huts and the odd plankwall dwelling in wooded regions. The depletion of the French forests had led to a replacement of wood by stone as a walling material. Timber was still used in contemporary France for flooring and roof frames, but its use had diminished since the early Middle Ages. In Canada, with its abundant forests, wood became the principal building material for all parts of the house from the foundation up.

The potential of timber in home construction was not fully appreciated by the first generation of immigrants from Europe. The earliest, widespread type of domestic house built by the French in Canada was the

The Rodrigue House at Louisbourg, where half-timbered (*colombage pierroté*) construction continued in the eighteenth century.

maison en colombage whose ancestor was the medieval, half-timbered house of northwestern Europe. Starting with a wooden frame, the builder placed closely-spaced studs or upright posts in the walls and then filled the intervening spaces with stone and mortar. This was termed *colombage pierroté* and examples of this technique can be found in Normandy and elsewhere in France. In Canada, where long and straight timbers were plentiful, the studs ran from sill to plate and there were fewer curved and diagonal pieces than would be found in French half-timbered walls. In 1644 Marie de L'Incarnation of the Ursulines described the houses of the colonists at Quebec as being "of framework filled with stone, two or three being also entirely of stone."[3] From this it appears that *colombage pierroté* was the dominant mode of construction at that settlement. Half-timber buildings were common in eighteenth century Louisbourg which, thanks to the seasonal fishery, had continuous contact with western France. There brick was also used as a fill between the timbers. *Colombage bousillé* employed a cheap fill of stone with mud or clay and was well known in seventeenth century New France. A similar fill sandwiched between parallel walls of boards made up the walls of buildings erected in 1639 at the Jesuit mission of Sainte-Marie-aux-Hurons near Lake Huron.[4] This was

24

The upright posts were closely spaced in *Canadien* half-timbering (*colombage*).

exceptional. Private *colombage* houses with a stone and mortar fill could dispense with wall boards which, because they were hand-sawn in the 1600s, were expensive. The phrase "maison couverte de planches" is frequently used in documents of the period and it has been misinterpreted as meaning weather-boarding on the walls;[5] it refers to the board roofs that were common in the colony. Protective boarding over stone walls appeared at a much later date. Like the newly-arrived immigrant who inhabited it, the *colombage* or half-timbered house was a European type transplanted to the New World. The full adaptation of form and building technique to the new land had not yet been made.

One of the earliest building contracts made in New France was that concluded in January, 1640, between Jean Bourdon, an engineer from Normandy, and Martin Grouvel, a carpenter of the Quebec region. Quebec

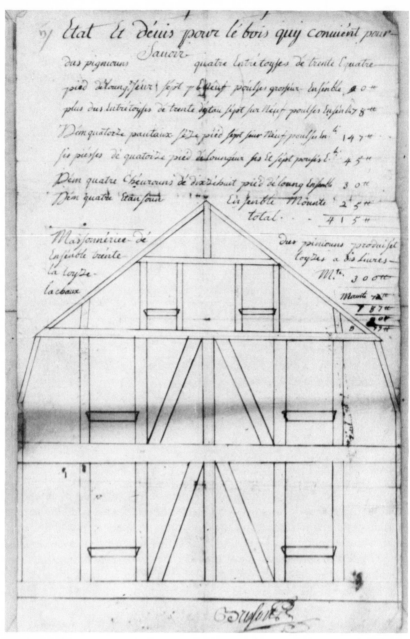

Specifications and plan for a half-timbered gable for a house with a gambrel or mansard roof, drawn in 1752 by Michel Dubenca, a Louisbourg carpenter.

was the first permanent French settlement on the St. Lawrence River and it served as a base for subsequent expansion into the interior of North America. Bourdon engaged the carpenter to build him a home and a barn on his estate near the village of Quebec. In the contract Grouvel promised to erect "a habitable house whose exterior length would be 32 *pieds*, and which would be 18 *pieds* across on the inside with a partition wall down the middle . . . [with] a fireplace and chimney at both ends of the said dwelling in which there will also be a cellar." The studs in this *colombage* house were to be at least six *pouces* square and five to six *pouces* apart with a plaster and rubble fill between them. This fill would be six *pouces* thick.[6] The customary spacing of the vertical posts in Canadian half-timbered construction was six to eight *pouces* and a distance of one *pied* between the uprights was not unknown. The same *colombage* technique would be used for the gable above the plate, a beam that tied the top of the wall together, when gables were required. In the late seventeenth century some houses with solid timber walls were built with *colombage* gables – a memento of the older style of building.

Half-timber construction is documented in the Quebec area from the 1630s onward and it spread to the upriver settlements of Trois-Rivières and Montreal in the following decades. To judge from the building contracts, *colombage* did not achieve the same dominance in these later settlements. At Quebec it was firmly established and, with the exception of Louisbourg, it lingered there the longest before being abandoned. A recently-discovered *colombage* house in Rimouski-Est indicates that the technique held on until the late eighteenth century in a few areas of the St. Lawrence valley.[7] Examples of two storey houses of *colombage* could be found in the town of Quebec in the late 1600s. One, built for the stonemason Jean Maillou in 1690, had a cedar frame and a second floor *galerie* or covered walk facing the river. The attic storey may have provided additional living space since the contract provided for a knee wall two *pieds* high above the second floor ceiling joists.[8] This was a well-used device for creating living quarters in the attic and, if it were too cold up there in winter for the owner, it was deemed sufficiently warm for children or servants. At Quebec, half-timbered dwellings slowly disappeared in the eighteenth century. The technique was not abandoned all at once; *colombage* was retained for a time as a cheap substitute for solid stone in the foundations of a few wooden houses and some later buildings of timber and stone were constructed with *colombage* gables and partition walls. An example of the gradual transition from *colombage pierroté* to stone in the town of Quebec was the home of Joachim Girard, a shoemaker. The facade of the ground floor was masonry and in 1713 Girard employed a carpenter to erect a second storey on this base *en colombage*. The front was a pretentious sham: the roof was a mansard on the street face, which was fashionable in the late 1600s, and yet it was straight at the back. In contrast with stone facade, the back wall of the ground floor was a miserable assemblage of plain wooden posts. These the shoemaker hoped to replace with stone "eventually."[9]

Outside of Quebec there was not a simple transference from half-timbering to masonry construction; the trend was towards entirely wood houses. The appearance of a third and increasingly-popular type of dwelling was signalled by Pierre Boucher's *Histoire Veritable et Naturelle* in 1664. To the question "of what are the houses built" in Canada?, Boucher replied, "Some are built entirely of stone, and are roofed with pine boards or shakes; others are of *colombage*, that is, framed and then filled with masonry between the timbers; others still are built wholly of wood and are roofed, as I have said, with boards."[10] In comparison with the full timber house, half-timber dwellings made little sense in New France. For the

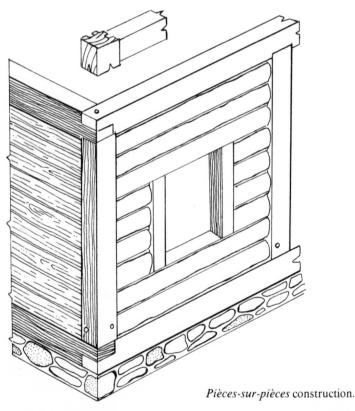

Pièces-sur-pièces construction.

28

Europeans rubble and plaster fill or clay and straw was an economic replacement for the wood that was in declining supply. Half-timbering seems to have evolved from entirely wood, framed buildings such as those that can still be found in Scandinavia. In Canada, however, there was no want of good building timber and, it might be noted, wood is a better insulator against the cold than stone or rubble. The extreme temperature changes in New France would also destroy the bonding of fill and timber and cause the wall to disintegrate. If we assume that half-timbered buildings evolved in Europe from a completely wooden type, then it can be said that builders in the colony reversed the trend in the second half of the seventeenth century. In the Canadian countryside the *maison en colombage* was superseded by the solid wooden house built in a manner that was distinctive of New France.

The new method of wood construction spread quickly in the Montreal region in the 1660s and 1670s. Ville-Marie de Montréal had been founded in 1642 and was 170 miles upriver from Quebec. Since it was still

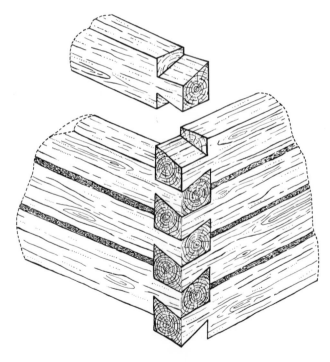

Dovetailing in house construction was known in the French regime but did not come into extensive use until the nineteenth century.

at the colonizing stage, it was an area receptive to innovation. It also appears that suitable building stone was more difficult to obtain than it was at Quebec. The new technique of building was called *pièces de bois sur pièces de bois*, which was soon shortened to *pièces-sur-pièces*. The apparent transition from framed *colombage* was quite simple: the stone and mortar fill between the upright posts was replaced by wood so that one had an entire wall of vertical posts that were dressed on two sides or fully squared. In a later and unrecorded transition the wooden infill went from the vertical to the horizontal.

On Ile-Royale (Cape Breton) vertical fill walls coexisted with horizontal *pièces-sur-pièces* and they persisted as the dominant type of timber construction. In a description of the government buildings at Port Dauphin on the island in 1715 it was said of the magazine, bakery and forge that "these buildings are made *pièces-sur-pièces*. These are short beams that are placed one on top of another, and whose ends are slotted into other upright posts placed at intervals of 10 *pieds*. Such buildings last from 40 to 50 years." The spacing of the grooved uprights into which the horizontal members were slotted was double the distance that was customary. Nearby the workers were building a barracks built with "a timber frame whose supporting posts are 10 *pieds* apart. The empty spaces between them are filled with upright pieces of wood."[11] The vertical fill consisted of round posts or *piquets* that were chinked and plastered over with roughcasting. *Piquets*, whether framed or planted directly into the ground, were the hallmark of the French fishing communities on Newfoundland and Cape Breton.[12]

In conventional *pièces-sur-pièces*, as known in the St. Lawrence valley, the horizontal timbers were fully squared and a tenon or tongue was made at each end which fitted into a vertical groove in the upright posts of the frame. The mortise thus formed was sometimes secured with a wooden pin as were the joints in the frame. Retention by tongue and groove, called *poteaux en coulisse*, was the standard form of assemblage. The corners of the house were occasionally secured by dovetailing the horizontal timbers rather than by fitting them into the corner post. The intervening bays of the wall in such a house were held together by the more conventional tongue-and-groove technique. Dovetailing (*à queue d'aronde*) the corners of *pièces-sur-pièces* barns and houses became widespread in nineteenth century French Canada and this change might be attributed to the influence of the English speaking immigrants from other parts of North America. Dovetailing was a common method of putting together squared log buildings in the English colonies. The *Canadiens* used the technique for walling before the British conquest of New France in 1760; witness a

The Ross House (1854) is in Manitoba where *pièces-sur-pièces* construction was naturalized as "Red River Frame."

This *piquet* hut was typical of the rough dwellings built in the French fishing settlements of Newfoundland and Cape Breton.

1714 building contract made at Quebec for " a 20 *pieds* square house of dovetailed *pièces-sur-pièces.*"[13] From the documents, however, it appears that the French colonials favoured their own indigenous method of wood construction.[14]

The framed upright posts that were in general use in Acadia were known as *pieux* or *poteaux sur sole* in the rest of New France where they were sometimes used for domestic housing. It was not a common building technique in the St. Lawrence valley. One client in 1667 apparently had it in mind when he instructed his carpenter to "enclose the said house with upright pieces of wood."[15] As late as 1748 a carpenter living near Montreal agreed to erect "a house [. . .] on sills enclosed by squared wooden posts; the same to be entirely built of cedarwood."[16] Round posts or squared timbers planted in the ground (*pieux* or *poteaux en terre*) have been described as a common feature of housebuilding in New France. While this may be true for Acadia and the settlements of the Upper Mississippi, it is not applicable to the area now known as the Province of Quebec. Barns and stables were built in this manner, but it was regarded as unsuitable for a permanent human shelter. Such a structure would have an earthen floor and the posts, being in constant contact with damp soil, decayed rapidly. Horizontal and framed *pièces-sur-pièces* became the preferred method for constructing wooden houses in central New France. From there, the French-speaking employees of the fur-trading companies carried this technique in the nineteenth century across western Canada where it was known as "Red River Frame." Thanks to the Hudson's Bay Company, some of the best surviving examples of *pièces-sur-pièces* construction are to be found in the Province of British Columbia, over 3,000 miles from the technique's homeland.

Pièces-sur-pièces was popular because it was superior to *colombage* and the wall of vertical timbers. The latter provided good insulation and water would drain easily from a wall of upright posts. However, when the timbers were laid upon one another horizontally, the chinking of moss, cedar bark, clay or plaster was less likely to fall out and the building would remain weathertight. Imagine as well the consequences of the shrinkage and warping of the wood that would occur over time. The vertical posts in a frame would tend to fall out and the entire wall, if not firmly pegged, might collapse. In a conventional *pièces-sur-pièces* wall, shrinkage would cause the squared logs to settle without being dislodged. With temperature changes the tenonned timbers would expand and contract with the entire frame, making it a durable structure in the harsh Canadian climate. There were other practical features that would appeal to the thrifty *Canadien*.

EXPLICATION DE LA PLANCHE XVIII.

Outils de Charpenterie.

1 Grande Regle.
2 Petite Regle platte.
3 Grand Compas.
4 Petit Compas.
5 Couteau.
6 Niveau.
7 Niveau à plomb plein.
8 Niveau à plomb percé.
9 Calibre.
10 Equaire.
11 Fausse Equaire.
12 Equaire de bois à Epaulement.

13 Sauterelle.
14 Scie à refendre.
15 Scie à débiter.
16 Esbauchoir.
17 Jauge à tracer les Mortaises
18 Besaigue.
19 Ciseau à manche de bois, avec Virolles.
20 Autre Ciseau.
21 Amorçoir.
22 Laceret ou petit Tariere.
23 Gros Tariere.

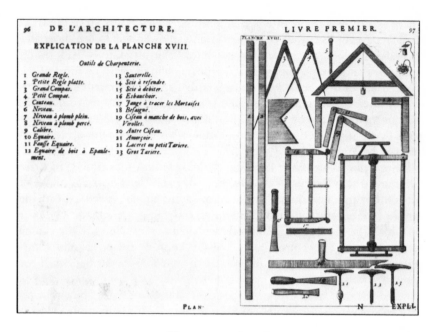

The carpenter's tools.

EXPLICATION DE LA PLANCHE XIX.

Suite des Outils de Charpenterie.

1 Maillets gros & mediocres.
2 Marteau de fer.
3 Petite Coignée à grand manche pour abatre le bois, & ébaucher.
4 Grande Coignée à équarir. Il y en a encore d'autres de diverses grandeurs.
5 Hachette à marteau.
6 Traceret.

7 Roinete.
8 Cheville de fer pour assembler.
9 Repoussoir.
10 Rabot rond.
11 Gallere.
12 Herminette.
13 Leviers.
14 Pinces.
15 Pied-de-Chevre.

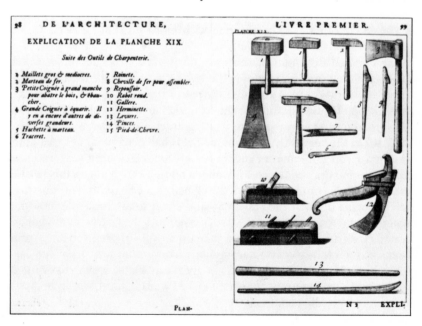

There was little wastage of wood in building such a house since the standard spacing of five *pieds* between uprights allowed one to use short and irregular sections of timber for the infill. The ultimate consideration would be that a single man with a few portable tools could do most of the work of building himself and, since boards needed two men and a whipsaw for their manufacture, one could get by with a temporary roof of tree bark or thatch. It can be assumed that many *pièces-sur-pièces* homes were built by do-it-yourself colonists and others without making a notarized contract beforehand.

Since a *pièces-sur-pièces* dwelling could be built for less than 250 *livres* currency, it was the customary dwelling of rural *Canadiens* and those of modest fortune. The clients' concern for saving money is revealed by the terms of the contracts for wooden houses; economies were made wherever possible. The carpenter was usually engaged to provide only his skilled labour and the client provided all of the building materials and transported them to the foundation which, in most cases, he had built for himself. It was also the rule in Canada that when an artisan was employed at some distance from his home the client would feed him. The employer or a helper supplied by him would be present to dress the timber and to help the carpenter raise the frame. The country folk, according to Intendant Gilles Hocquart, "all handle the axe with skill"[17] and they could have done much of the rough carpentry by themselves. The "carpenter" might, in fact, be another farmer, but one with more skill and experience in woodworking.

The detailed examples of seventeenth century construction in wood come from the Montreal region in the 1670s because it was in the countryside of this newly-settled area that the *pièces-sur-pièces* house had its greatest impact. House building in the Montreal area was closely related to the agricultural seasons and our first contract was made in November, 1673, when the harvest was in and the fields had been ploughed. Autumn was an appropriate time for making plans for the coming year and, indeed, most building contracts for wooden houses were made in this season and in the early winter. Contracting well before the beginning of construction in spring allowed the craftsman and client to assemble the building materials and to clear the work site. This permitted construction to get off to a quick start without interfering with the sowing of grains in late April. There was wisdom too in obtaining an early commitment from the carpenter since local craftsmen were not always available when you wanted them. Only a small number of clients risked waiting until March or April to draw up a building contract.

The builder of our first example of a *pièces-sur-pièces* house was Etienne

Trudeau, a well-established houseframer whose descendants are not unknown. His employer was a more recent arrival from France named Barthélemy Vinet, called la Rente. Vinet was both a farmer and a limeburner. The two had discussed the matter before going to Bénigne Basset, the principal notary in the town of Ville-Marie de Montréal, to have the agreement put into writing. Under their *marché*, Trudeau promised "to construct for Vinet a *pièces-sur-pièces* dwelling on his land grant at Lachine; the said house to be 23 *pieds* long on the outside and 20 *pieds* wide, also on the exterior, and 10 *pieds* high at the corners." No date was set for beginning construction since it was generally understood that wooden houses were begun in late March when one could again work out of doors in comfort. The size of the house was typical of *pièces-sur-pièces* houses in the Montreal region during the late seventeenth century: the average length was between 18 and 26 *pieds*. A common ratio of length to depth was 5:4. The exterior wall height of ten *pieds* was exactly the norm; walls could be as high as twelve *pieds* and as low as six *pieds*. This would result in a low ceiling for us, but there would be no bruised foreheads for the people of the seventeenth century who were just over five feet tall.

The roof structure of Vinet's one-storey house will remain a mystery, for the contract specified that it be "a roof frame of the same construction as that on Jean-Baptiste Gadoys' house." And should we locate the contract for the Gadoys house, we might find that its roof was to copy that of yet another building. Clauses that directed the builder to imitate such-and-such a feature on the house of so-and-so are commonplace in the contracts. It made things perfectly clear to the craftsman and entirely baffling to subsequent generations. Trudeau was to provide transverse joists (*Sollivaux passans*) for the floor and ceiling, a mantel for the fireplace, and *colombage* gables. This last feature reminds us that the transition from full *colombage* to full *pièces-sur-pièces* was not complete. The provision that the framing timbers be dressed "sur les quatre faces" also recalls the earlier period when tree trunks would be only partially dressed to provide a shelter as cheaply and as quickly as possible. Until the conclusion of a treaty of peace and neutrality in 1701, the Iroquois Amerindians raided Montreal Island and the outlying settlements. The 1650s and 1660s were, in particular, a time of fear and haste: a carpenter demanded armed protection on the job[18] and one settler had a projection with defensive loopholes built into his house.[19] The reinforcement of the colony with regular troops and more immigrants meant that the 1670s were less anxious times. Vinet's house was to be "ready for roofing at the end of July" in 1674. This was ample time, for a wooden house begun in March could easily be finished by June.

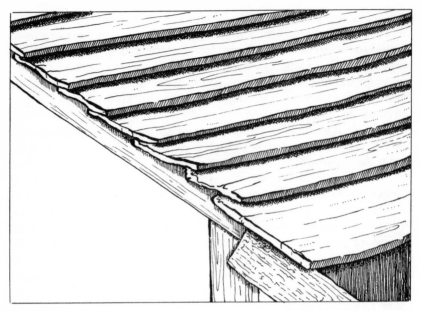

Overlapping boards (*planches chevauchées*) were commonly used to roof rural houses.

The Trudeau-Vinet contract did not mention foundations, floors, a chimney or the roof covering. Trudeau, who was the son of a mason, could have made a stone foundation and the chimney as well as the body of the house. It is more likely, however, that Vinet provided these for himself and of less durable materials. The floors would have been made of cedar or pine boards butted. The roof was most certainly one of boards laid over the rafters; they could have been overlapping and horizontal to the eaves (*chevauchées*), board and batten, or laid in two layers. Chimneys at this time were wattle-and-daub (*bousillage*) and these gave way to masonry chimneys at the end of the seventeenth century.

Barthélemy Vinet explicitly bound himself "to transport by cart each and every timber of the said building, when they have been squared, to the location chosed for the said building whenever Truteau (sic) needs them." An indication of Vinet's lack of ready cash is the form of payment: the carpenter was to be recompensed with 52 hogsheads (*barriques*) of burnt lime from Vinet's lime kiln at Côte Saint-Joseph and he was to enjoy the use of a small *logis* to be built by the client in 1674.[20] The poorer *habitants* would pay the builder with produce, such as grain, or with reciprocal services if the craftsman would accept them. In contemporary contracts we find a carpenter paid with a five-year lease on a piece of farmland with its barn,[21] and the framer of a *pièces-sur-pièces* house repaid by having the customer build him a *colombage* dwelling![22] The townspeople of Louisbourg had their own unique form of payment: the builder of the dwelling would be allowed the use of the house and lot for a number of years.[23]

The omissions in the Trudeau-Vinet contract make it hard to visualize the house, and so we shall supplement it with details taken from another agreement to build a similar house. This second deed was made in August, 1674, at Montreal between Pierre Verrier, called la Saulaye, "carpenter and settler on the said Island [of Montreal]," and Pierre Richomme, a farmer, and his wife. Verrier was an indifferent workman who, earlier in the year, had been charged with having built a barn roof with inadequate bracing and weak joints.[24] On this occasion he agreed with Richomme to construct "at one end of the bake-oven belonging to the house that was formerly on the land grant – a dwelling of *pièces de bois sur pièces*, 20 *pieds* long on the outside by 18 *pieds* wide, also on the outside, and [with walls] 9 *pieds* high." It was clearly the farmer's intention to continue using his old bake oven. The fate of his former home on the site is not mentioned. When one house was to replace another on the same location the *Canadiens* salvaged as much as they could from the old structure. Sound timbers would be re-used and the ironwork was always retrieved because of its high value. A country house would have, at least, iron hinges for the doors, shutters and casement windows, as well as bolts to secure them. Richomme's old residence could have been stripped of its windows and hardware and be left standing for use as a stable or outbuilding. A nearby *pièces-sur-pièces* house was dismantled that very year to be reconstructed as a barn in another place.[25]

The roof frame of the new Richomme house was to copy that of the house of "the one called Le Houx" built in the common. On the matter of floors, ceilings and openings this contract was more specific: "Three joists for the ceiling and two beams over the cellar . . . . An opening for one door, and two windows as well as a mantelpiece, with butted joints; the sills to be of oak or of butternut wood (*noyer tendre*) and the remainder of the frame to be of hemlock (*bois pruches*)."[26] Like so many others of the French regime, this house would have been built on rising ground overlooking the river. Near the town of Montreal the river side would also give the front of the building a southerly exposure. This was always preferred in country houses because the front received the warmth of the sun for most of the day. With this orientation, the back of the dwelling received the prevailing northeasterly wind. This, too, was desirable, especially in winter. At least the door and one window would be on the southern face of this house and the other was likely in the western wall. The chimney

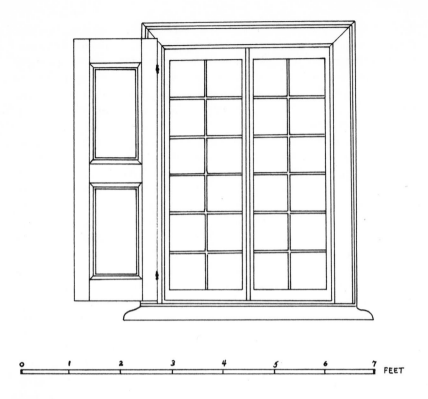

0 1 2 3 4 5 6 7 FEET

A window from the outside with a shutter in place. Such casement windows are typical of French architecture.

would then be located in the other end. Other houses in the area had, on the average, four windows and one or two doors. For a farmer, oiled paper rather than glass filled the window sash.[27] Fenestration in French Canadian homes increased dramatically in the nineteenth century with the availability of cheap glass panes. The choice of woods for the framework of the Richomme house was exceptional: sills were customarily of cedar and not, as here, of oak or butternut because cedar was most resistant to damp rot. The stipulation that the rest of the frame be of hemlock (*pruche*)[28] was more conventional; ash, spruce, beech and even cedar were used in New France for making the framework of a wooden house from the sills up. Oak, ash (*frêne*) and hemlock were the preferred woods.

We are now in a position to follow the building of *pièces-sur-pièces* house in the seventeenth century from start to finish. When a contract was concluded before a notary, say, in autumn, it was then the custom to seal the accord with a libation. This drink was called the *vin de marché* or the *pot-de-vin*, though in Canada the drink was usually hard liquor. Payments to the builders included a few *pots* or half-gallon measures of *eau-de-vie* and it is clear that, in the early years of the colony, the brandy was downed when the contract was approved and a small advance paid to the housewright. The evidence is a court case in 1680 in which a contractor, who had not begun work on the date agreed, was charged one *livre* for the "two *pots* of wine that were drunk when the agreement was made."[29] In the building of the chapel at Sainte-Anne de Beaupré in 1661 the *pot* was given to the carpenter when the first peg was driven into the frame.[30] By the second half of the seventeenth century the custom of the gratuitous *pot-de-vin* was losing ground and its meaning became confused. Witness two Quebec contracts of the 1680s, one of which called for "a hat worth one gold *pistole* for the *vin du marché*"[31] while the other specified "one *pistole* for the gift hat once the framework is complete."[32] The idea that one gave the craftsman something as a good-will gesture lingered and in the eighteenth century bonuses were infrequently given upon the completion of the contract. This practice might have been equally inspired by the leave-taking gifts given to faithful servants and, like the gifts, the bonus took the form of shoes, clothes, some food perhaps, or a useful object like a tool. The more extraordinary rewards given to building craftsmen included a bushel (*minot*) of shellfish,[33] two pounds of steel,[34] and 50 eels.[35]

In the winter, following the conclusion of the contract, the client cut the timber with, on one occasion, having the carpenters assist their employer in locating trees suitable for beams.[36] If the carpenter were to cut the timber, he would usually be directed to take it off the client's land. This right was open to abuse, for the artisan might cut a few extra trees for his own use and client and craftsman might not be able to resist the temptation of felling a few fine trees on a neighbour's property. The fallen trees were ordinarily dressed in the woods before being transported to the building site, possibly on a sledge drawn by oxen or horses. It is remarkable that builders in the seventeenth century rarely used seasoned timber for house frames. They did take the precaution of cutting the trees in winter when they had the least sap in them. Seasoned boards would be used for flooring; one could imagine the pleasure of walking on green pine wood with the gum oozing out.

On the absence of a contemporary account of the construction sequence, we must rely on the observations of an American who watched French-Canadians building their homes in the Upper Great Lakes region during the early nineteenth century. "When the building is to be put up," wrote Sherman Hall, the timber of the sills, beams and posts is cut and hewed into suitable sticks, usually with a common axe, for a hewing broad axe is seldom seen here, and nobody knows how to use it. The sills and beams are generally locked, or halfed together at the corners of the building, for few can frame them together with tenant (sic) and mortice. A mortice is made in the sill for a post wherever it is needed and an other in the beam. A groove is made in each post from top to bottom about 2 inches in width, and three or four inches deep. Timbers are then hewed six or seven inches thick and the ends cut till they are fitted to the groove in the post, and of sufficient length to reach from one post to another. They are then introduced one after another till the walls of the building are completed . . . . Wherever a window or a door is required, posts are erected, into which the ends of the [horizontal] timbers are introduced, instead of the main posts, and thus the required hole is made in the wall. A post is placed at the centre of each end of the building which is continued above the beam as high as the top of the roof is intended to be. A stick of timber is then laid on top of these posts reaching from one end of the building to the other, and forms the ridge pole. The roof is then formed by laying one end of timbers on this ridge pole and the other on the plate till the whole is covered.[37]

It must be remembered that this describes the work of an amateur builder in a remote area and that in the St. Lawrence valley the houses had framed and jointed roofs as well as a more finished appearance. The procedure, however, would have been much the same and the craftsman, though working with a wider variety of tools, still had no plans save those in his head.

As the preparation of the frame for our seventeenth century farmhouse proceeded in March and April, the patron would, if he had not already done so, build the stone foundations needed to separate the wooden frame from the dampness of the ground. It was folly to lay the sills directly on the earth and, yet, a few people did this or contented themselves with a foundation of wood blocks or flat stones. If there were to be no cellar (*cave*), the stone foundations would only be two to three-and-a-half *pieds* high. Ideally, they should reach below the frost level in the ground to ensure a stable footing for the house. Because the foundations were usually the responsibility of the client, they are not well documented in the building contracts for wooden houses. Most, it seems, were of stone and mortar and a small number were of *colombage*.

When the carpenter was not being paid in proportion to the work done (*au fur et à mesure*), the completion of the members of the frame was considered an appropriate time for making the second payment after the advance given at the signing of the contract. A few customers withheld all payment until this stage of construction. It was prudent to hold back a substantial portion of the total due until the very end in order to keep the carpenter on the job and to push him through the tedious stages of preparing the timber. The most satisfying moment came in late April when the foundations and all of the joints were finished. With a hand axe and then a mallet and chisel each tongue-like tenon had been cut at the end of the uprights to match the hollow mortises in the length of the sill and plate. Corresponding mortises and tenons were sometimes given a common marking as an *aide-memoire* for assemblage. After the sills were laid out on the foundations the posts were seated in their mortises and a slightly oversized, hardwood peg was driven into a hole that went through the entire joint to secure it. More than one man was required to shift the sills and to raise the plate beams, and so the client was obliged to supply his own labour or that of another to assist in erecting the frame. Farmers were anxious not to be diverted from sowing to aid in this work and one insisted that the house be completed "before the next seed-time."[38]

The demands of agriculture were also reflected in the completion dates for wooden houses in New France. Most of the buildings were to be completed before the end of June so that the parties would be free for haying in July and the grain harvest in August and September. There was a small concentration of completion dates in August, presumably between these two events.[39] September was, as they say in polite society, "impossible," for the harvest was then in full swing. When a Quebec builder was asked to clean up a boat-load of stone left near the building he had completed, he pointed out that it was September "and it was now the harvest break (*temps de vacance*) so that he cannot have it removed immediately because of the difficulty in obtaining transport." The court accepted his excuse and he was allowed to put off the cleanup until October when the harvest would be over.[40]

With two or three men, the raising of the house frame took very little time; it could be done in one or two days. Once the grooved uprights were firmly seated in the sill, the horizontal fill could be lowered into place, with allowance for a door and windows. With a standard spacing of five *pieds* between upright posts, there would be three or four bays on the front and back walls. The heaviest task was the lifting of the long wall plates whose mortises would fit over the tenons on the top of the posts and secure the entire length of the wall. Once in place, the plate would serve as a base for the roof trusses. The trusses could be assembled on the ground and then raised with ropes and poles. They were joined together by longitudinal

Croix de Sainte-André bracing in a roof-frame as seen from below.

braces and purlins and they sometimes received additional support from diagonal wind braces known as *croix de Saint-André*.

At this point, with the roof frame up, the walls and gables complete and the ceiling and floor joists in place, the carpenter was usually paid off and our *habitant* took over to finish the house. Up to this stage no nails had been used; the structure was held together by interlocking joints and wooden pegs. Using boards bought from a sawyer or that he had cut with another's help, the client nailed down the floor and roof covering. Hand-forged nails were expensive and they were used with economy; just two sufficed to tie the board to each rafter or joist. The most frequently-cited form of roofing was *planches chevauchées* or overlapping boards laid parallel to the eaves. A second layer of tongue-and-groove or plain boards lay underneath the overlapping boards on a number of roofs. This provided a more effective barrier against blowing snow and the cold. When wood shingles came into widespread use in the following century they were nailed to a layer of boards that covered the rafters. In the period under consideration the roofing and the installation of floors, doors, windows and partitions appears to have belonged to amateurs in the rural areas and it was, perforce, rough work.

The interior partitions of boards and, occasionally, of *colombage* created two functional divisions of space in the farmhouse: one for sleeping and the other for cooking and eating. This was the pattern observed by the Finnish botanist, Peter Kalm, when he visited New France in 1749.[41] The interior lay-out of the *Canadien* farmhouse in the St. Lawrence valley was described in greater detail by a German officer at Batiscan in 1776:

> In the interior the walls are covered with smoothly planed boards; likewise the ceiling [or upper floor] . . . . All the partitions of the house are built with wooden boards. For this reason, you will find the three following inconveniences. First: should any one be walking about the rooms, you will hear a slight creaking; secondly: should anyone be walking on the floor overhead, the one underneath would be in momentary expectation of having him drop down upon his head; and, thirdly: should one talk, every word can be heard, either in the next room or in the kitchen . . . . The kitchens are so clean that they are used as a 'living room' until the arrival of the cold weather . . . . Next to the kitchen is a room generally used as a sleeping room. Houses containing two [bed-] rooms are scarce; and when they contain *three* are considered very genteel.[42]

The writer described the exterior walls of these houses as "covered with lime or boards." The boards were an innovation since earlier *pièces-sur-pièces* houses were chinked with fibre and clay, sometimes covered with roughcast (*crépi* or *gobetage*), and were whitewashed all over with whiting of lime (*lait de chaux*). As for house paints for the interior or the exterior, there is no reference to them in the French regime and it must be assumed that the "typical" colour scheme of the French-Canadian house belongs to the nineteenth century.[43]

In the older, settled regions on the St. Lawrence River, masonry farmhouses made their appearance in large numbers during the eighteenth century. These buildings, being built of a more durable material, have outlasted many of their wooden contemporaries. The selectivity of survival has led to the mistaken assumption, based on what has endured, that the majority of farmhouses in New France were of stone. Undoubtedly, the longer the period of settlement and the greater the prosperity of the rural population, the more numerous would be the masonry structures. In New France, as one moved outward to the newly-settled areas, the stone houses disappeared and wooden dwellings, invariably *pièces-sur-pièces*, reigned supreme. This transition was noted by Peter Kalm as he travelled from Lake Champlain, through the fringe of settlement, to the long-established seigneuries on the St. Lawrence River. When, after his wilderness journey, he reached the first cultivated clearings north of Saint-Jean, he noted that "the houses are built of wood and are very small . . . , they employ clay for stopping up the crevices in the walls. The roofs are made very much sloping, and covered with straw."[44] Proceeding downriver

The Paradis House at Charlesbourg was a rare survivor of the wooden cottages of the French regime.

from Montreal Island to Quebec, Kalm passed through seigneuries that had been farmed for nearly a century and there he observed that "the farm-houses are generally built of stone, but sometimes of timber, and have three of four rooms. The windows are seldom of glass, but most frequently of paper . . . . The roofs are covered with boards."[45] This must have been one of the few areas where stone dwellings outnumbered those of wood or, perhaps, Kalm was deceived as he floated down the river by the wooden houses that were covered with roughcasting and whitewashed. After touring the *seigneuries* close to Quebec, the oldest in the colony and known to be fairly prosperous, and after a closer inspection he concluded that "the greater part of the houses in the country are built of wood, and sometimes plastered over on the outside."[46] Though he did not describe the mode of construction, these wooden farm houses were certainly built *pièces-sur-pièces.*

The *pièces-sur-pièces* house was, from the late seventeenth century to the late nineteenth century, the rural house of French Canada wherever the

Built at the beginning of the eighteenth century, this stone house at Cap Santé retains a French verticality while acknowledging the difficulties of life in Canada with two fireplaces and few windows.

trees were plentiful and the populace poor. In the nineteenth century it was carried into the newly-colonized Laurentian highlands and the Lac Saint-Jean region in the Province of Quebec where it was the first form of house built by the pioneers. From the primitive farmhouse of the seventeenth century developed the archetypal *Canadien* home of the early nineteenth century with its low-pitched roof and flared, projecting eaves that often extended into a verandah. The *pièces-sur-pièces* house, so well adapted to the resources and climate of the country, was one of the great creative innovations of French Canada.[47] It became part of the folk tradition of the people and it was not displaced by the log structures of the English-speaking settlers who came into the St. Lawrence valley after the conquest of New France in 1760. The *Canadiens* preferred their own, highly-successful method of building in wood.

NOTES

1. Gérard Morrisset, *L'Architecture en Nouvelle-France* (Quebec, 1949), 32-3; and repeated by Alan Gowans, *Images of American Living* (Philadelphia, 1964), 30, and others.
2. Louis Savot (F. Blondel ed.), *L'Architecture Françoise des Bastimens Particuliers* (Paris, 1685), 173.
3. Joyce Marshall (ed.), *Word from New France . . . Letters of Marie de L'Incarnation* (Toronto, 1967), 129
4. W. & E. M. Jury, *Sainte-Marie Among the Hurons*, 38-9, 76-7; Kenneth E. Kidd, *The Excavation of Sainte-Marie I* (Toronto, 1949), 38.
5. Ramsay Traquair, *The Old Architecture of Quebec* (Toronto, 1947), 66.
6. A.Q., G.N.R.F., M. Piraube, 29 jan. 1640.
7. Michel Lessard & Gilles Vilandré, *La Maison traditionnelle au Québec* (Montreal, 1974), 109-112, 323-341.
8. A.Q., G.N.R.F., F. Genaple, 10 déc. 1689.
9. A.Q., G.N.R.F., L. Chambalon, 2 avril 1713.
10. Pierre Boucher, *Histoire Veritable et Naturelle Des Moeurs & Productions du Pays de la Nouvelle France, Vulgairement dite Le Canada* (Paris, 1664), 140.
11. A.N., A.C., série C11B, I, ff.296-7.
12. Eric R. Krause, "Private Buildings in Louisbourg: 1713-1758," in *Canada, An Historical Magazine*, I:4 (June 1974), 47-59 The poverty of the records and the destruction the Acadian communities in 1755 and following years have robbed us of precise knowledge of *Acadien* housing on the mainland. French visitors such as Dièreville, author of *Relation du Voyage du Port Royal de l'Acadie* (1708), agree that the dwellings were rough, low wooden structures that were often roofed with thatch. The Acadians were renowned as carpenters and it is likely that these houses were framed; the intersices may have been filled with *piquets* or horizontal *pièces-sur-pièces*.
13. A.Q., G.N.R.F., L. Chambalon, 2 août 1714.
14. Since the French colonists knew of log structures with dovetailed corners, it might be conjectured that the English were equally aware of the wood-filled frame technique used in New France. Support for the belief that both forms of construction were known to the English seems to come from Pierre de Troyes' description in 1686 of the structures at Fort Albany and Moose Factory, which were built for the Hudson Bay Company, as "construit de pièces sur pièces." See Ivanhoë Caron (ed.), *Journal de L'Expedition du Chevalier de Troyes à la Baie d'Hudson en 1686* (Beauceville, 1918), 63-4, 89-90; this reference was supplied by George C. Ingram. I think it likely that de Troyes used this familiar phrase for horizontal timber structures whose corners were halved or dovetailed. Modern-day Acadians apply *pièces-sur-pièces* to all horizontal timber buildings. The archaeological excavation of Fort Albany under Walter A. Kenyon of the Royal Ontario Museum revealed that the main dwelling was "built of 18-inch squared timbers with half-lap joints at the corners. Each of the corners was fastened with three monstrous hand-wrought spikes." See W. A. Kenyon and J. R. Turnbull, *The Battle for James Bay 1686* (Toronto, 1971), 123.
15. A.Q., G.N.R.F., R. Becquet, 16 oct. 1667.

16. Archives du Québec (Montréal) [hereafter A.Q.M.], G.N.R.F., J.B. Adhémar, 25 sept. 1748.
17. P.A.C., C11A transcript, LXVII, 40-1.
18. A.Q.M., G.N.R.F., B. Basset, 6 oct. 1665.
19. A.Q.M., G.N.R.F., B. Basset, 4 mars 1663. It has been suggested that the Iroquois threat encouraged the construction of masonry houses with thick walls and small windows in the Montreal area. There is no documentary support for this assertion.
20. A.Q.M., G.N.R.F., B. Basset, 12 nov. 1673.
21. A.Q.M., G.N.R.F., B. Basset, 19 août 1674.
22. A.Q.M., G.N.R.F., T. Frérot, 27 sept. 1674.
23. A.N., A.C., série G3 (Notariat de Louisbourg), carton 2041-1, Nos.126 (30 mars 1751), 130 (6 oct. 1752), 144 (11 sept. 1752).
24. A.Q.M., G.N.R.F., B. Basset, 5 mars 1674 (Report of two carpenters on the barn roof built by Pierre Verrier for Étienne Campeau).
25. A.Q.M., G.N.R.F., B. Basset, 10 déc. 1673.
26. A.Q.M., G.N.R.F., B. Basset, 19 août 1674. The original reads "Trois sollivaux, Au plancher d'en haut et deux poutres à la cave . . . ; Une ouverture d'une porte & deux fenestres et son manteau de cheminée, à joints quarrez, savoir les solles de chesne ou noyer tendre et le reste de bois pruches."
27. Robert-Lionel Séguin, *La Maison en Nouvelle-France* (Ottawa, 1968), 41-3, states that paper window panes *replaced* glass panes in the Montreal region by the eighteenth century. The matter probably needs more research. Louisbourg, with its good maritime connections with France, was always well supplied with window glass. Glass was never manufactured in New France; it had to be imported.
28. *Pruche* usually means *tsuga canadensis* or hemlock; on Ile-Royale (Cape Breton) *pruche* or *prusse* was used for spruce.
29. A.Q.M., Juridiction de Montréal [hereafter J.M.], Bailliages 1665-1682, ff.348vo.
30. Lucien Gagné and Jean-Pierre Asselin (Eric W. Gosling trans.), *Saint Anne de Beaupré, Pilgrim's Goal for Three Hundred Years* (Ste Anne de Beaupré, 1967), 9.
31. A.Q., G.N.R.F., G. Rageot, 24 mai 1686.
32. A.Q., G.N.R.F., F. Genaple, 30 mai 1684.
33. A.Q., G.N.R.F., L. Chambalon, 28 mars 1700.
34. A.Q., G.N.R.F., J. E. Dubreuil,24 fév. 1714.
35. A.Q., G.N.R.F., C. Barolet, 3 avril 1748.
36. A.Q., G.N.R.F., G. Audouart, 4 déc. 1650.
37. Sherman Hall at Lac du Flambeau, Wisconsin, to Aaron Hall, Sept. 20th 1832; quoted in Grace Lee Nute, *The Voyageur* (St. Paul, 1955), 189-90. This letter was brought to my attention by A. "Jack" Richardson.
38. A.Q.M., G.N.R.F., B. Basset, 11 fév. 1660.
39. Of thirty contracts for wooden houses which set the completion date, fifteen required completion before the end of June and seven selected August as the month in which the house was to be finished.
40. P.A.C., M.G. 8, B1, IX, 354-5 (6 sept. 1707).
41. Peter Kalm (J. R. Forster trans.), *Travels into North America*. 4 vols. (London, 1771), III, 163, 256.

42. W. L. Stone (ed.), *Letters of Brunswick and Hessian Officers during the American Revolution* (Albany, 1891), 16-8. This reference was kindly supplied by A. "Jack" Richardson of the federal Historic Sites Branch.

43. On the "typical" colour scheme of the French-Canadian house, see Ramsay Traquair, *The Old Architecture of Quebec*, 59.

44. Peter Kalm, III, 51.

45. Peter Kalm, III, 79-80

46. Peter Kalm, III, 159.

47. To say that *pièces-sur-pièces* construction was an indigenous development is not to say that it was without precedent. Harold R. Shurtleff wrote of a walling system in which horizontal planks were fitted into upright posts with grooved sides; this system, he said, "was common for barns and storehouses throughout Northern Europe and the British Isles." See H.R. Shurtleff, *The Log Cabin Myth* (Cambridge Mass., 1939), 76. Scandinavian stave churches of the 11th and 12th centuries were framed and had vertical plank walls that were rabbetted into the corner posts; this could have been the ancestor of the technique described by Shurtleff. See Guthorm Kavli, *Norwegian Architecture Past and Present* (Oslo, n.d.), 15-16. Cultural diffusionists, who reject the possibility of independent innovation, will be disappointed to learn that there was no communication between New France and the parts of Northern Europe where plankwall construction was known. The *Canadiens*, however, moved to plankwalling in the nineteenth century as the supply of timber declined.

3

From Wood To Stone

In the largest towns of New France, wood did not yield to stone until the eighteenth century and the victory was far from complete. At Quebec, the administrative centre and fashion leader of the colony, contracts for masonry buildings appeared in rapidly increasing numbers from the 1680s onward. There was a slack period at the beginning of the eighteenth century due, no doubt, to the war and hardship of the times. In 1720 Father Charlevoix signalled the transformation of the old capital: "Almost all the houses are built of stone, which is remarkable, considering that the town contains only about 7,000 souls."[1] There is hyperbole in this, for the town contained scarcely 3,000 persons and only half the private houses could have been built of stone. Of 83 houses enumerated in 1737 and 1739, 46 or 55% were of masonry construction. The remainder were framed houses, usually *pièces-sur-pièces*, and only eight were of *colombage*, which had once been the dominant form of construction in Quebec.[2] The other towns were slow to follow. Trois-Rivières always remained a village of wooden houses. Even at Louisbourg, that magnificent fortress-town on the Atlantic, timber housing was the rule. In 1745 a resident wrote that "for the most part the houses there are of wood, those of stone have been built at the king's expense."[3] At Montreal masonry buildings, aided by conflagrations and official pressure, took hold in the second quarter of the eighteenth century. In 1704 three-quarters of the houses built there were *pièces-sur-pièces*;[4] by 1731 just over half of the houses at Montreal identified by construction in the *aveu et denombrement* of the island were made of stone.[5] Some of the structures in Montreal and Quebec were hybrids with a ground floor of masonry construction and an upper storey of *pièces-sur-pièces*. In the 1750s a large proportion of the residences in Montreal were still partially or wholly built of wood.

Masonry houses in the towns of New France belonged to a world far removed from the wooden country cottage. The evolution of the rural dwelling was, until 1745, unhampered by official regulations. Builders in the countryside could proceed as they wished, provided the result satisfied the client. In the towns, as we have seen, construction was always subject to the rules of the *Coûtume de Paris* and the judiciary began to enforce these usages as well as laws of their own devising with greater zeal. As an example of this trend, we might note that although article 193 of the *Coûtume* required the householders of Paris to have "adequate latrines and privies," the rule was not applied in Canada until 1673. It was then incorporated into Governor Buade de Frontenac's "règlements de police" for the town of Quebec. Application extended to all future and existing houses "to avert the infection and stench that such filth occasions when people are allowed to deposit it in the streets."[6] The regulation was reissued in 1676 by the *Conseil souverain* at Quebec with the proviso "if the location of the houses permits it."[7] The latitude given to builders and residents by this qualification was too great, and in February, 1706, the council ordered all owners and tenants to add a privy to their current residence by springtime or be fined 20 *livres* for noncompliance. Builders were also forbidden to construct any dwelling in the future without a latrine.[8] In the summer of that year the *Conseil supérieur*, as it was now called, ordered a second inspection of the houses in Quebec. The council felt that the *Prévôté* officials had been too lenient in enforcing the law. The second inspection had its effect; twenty-three residents besieged the council with petitions begging to be exempted from the law.[9] The next problem for the authorities would be to get the Quebeckers to empty their new latrines once they were full and overflowing.[10]

The principal objective of building regulations for the towns of New France was not the preservation of street alignments or sanitation; it was protection against fires. The concern was proportionate to the danger. Fire was the scourge of Canadian towns and it spread rapidly through the timber houses and across cedar shingle roofs. At the first alarm the carpenters and joiners of Quebec were obliged "to go to the fire, axe in hand" to demolish adjoining structures while the citizenry fought the fire with buckets of water and grappling hooks to wrench off the burning roof.[11] Firefighters in this period could not hope to put out a large fire; they could only prevent it from spreading to other buildings, and they were not very effective at this. The Lower Town was, despite their efforts, razed by fire in 1682, and Montreal suffered major conflagrations in 1721, 1734 and 1754. Trois-Rivières was levelled by flames in 1752 and, as a consequence, barns, stables and the storage of hay were forbidden inside that town.[12]

The Jacquet House at Quebec was built in the late seventeenth century when masonry dwellings appeared in the town in increasing numbers.

The stimulus for the first building law aimed at fire prevention came from a notary's complaint to the Quebec *Conseil souverain* in 1673. He claimed that a nearby toolmaker's forge imperilled his documents and registers. This complaint led to the enforcement of those articles of the *Coûtume de Paris* requiring fire breaks and to some commonsense precautions against the hazards of particular forges in the town of Quebec.[13] Frontenac's public order regulations of March, 1673, included articles which forbade forges in private homes and ordered those metal-workers in the town who did not possess a forge and chimney built of stone to relocate their smithies to Côte de la Montagne road.[14] Ironworkers did eventually gravitate to this location between the Upper and Lower Towns as much, it seems, because of the updraft at the cliff face as because of

51

A country hearth on Ile d'Orléans with a heavy stone lintel and a wooden cooking crane.

official persuasion. The 1673 regulations for Quebec also demanded that new buildings in the closely-packed Lower Town be constructed with two stone gables to prevent the lateral spread of fire to adjacent houses.[15]

Of all the parts of town houses, the authorities in New France lavished the most attention on chimneys. The flues were to be swept every two months and householders in Quebec and Montreal were fined for chimney fires. Ladders were to be installed on every roof to facilitate the work of the sweeps, who were often roofers too. In the 1680s the *Conseil souverain*, under the presidency of Intendant Bochart de Champigny, set the standard dimensions of chimneys in the towns of the colony at three-and-

The Sifroy-Roy House at Beaumont is sheathed in boards to protect its masonry walls from moisture and frost.

a-half *pieds* above the roof crest with a flue ten *pouces* wide.[16] Any sparks that flew up the chimney would be extinguished by the time they settled on a roof. It was understood that the chimneys would be built of stone and mortar, and this was made explicit when the regulation was extended to Montreal.[17] In 1727 the minimum dimensions for a flue were more precisely defined as ten *pouces* by three *pieds*. The size of the flues was legislated so that they would be "of sufficient breadth to permit a sweep to pass through in order to clean them."[18] The officials, alas, had no control over the dimensions of the chimney-sweeps and in 1729 they were forced to request the dispatch of replacements from France because the two previously sent were now "too plump to get into the chimneys."[19]

The legal specifications for chimneys in the towns were constantly refined: flues were to be fully plastered in the interior and no piece of wood was to be attached to the chimney.[20] In 1749 a local ordinance for Montreal mentioned brick as an alternative lining for the flue.[21] Evidence that these laws were enforced comes from the building contracts which stipulate that the chimney to be built will be of the height prescribed by the *Conseil souverain* in 1688.[22] It is apparent from the court records that magistrates in Montreal, Quebec and Louisbourg were quick to respond

The Du Calvet House (1731)
at Montreal was separated from
its neighbours by heavy fire gables.

54

when a chimney fire had occurred or a complaint was lodged about a chimney that was in poor repair. Quebec always set the pace in building legislation and the 1727 regulations for chimneys were better enforced there than elsewhere in the colony. The *architecte du Roi*, a new official who served as the deputy Overseer of Highways within Quebec, acted as an inspector of chimneys in the eighteenth century. In 1729, 1744 and 1748 a complete survey was made of the town and those with faulty chimneys were prosecuted.[23] As *architecte du Roi*, Dominique Janson, called La Palme, drew up elaborate specifications for the construction of chimneys at Quebec and these rules were given legal force by the *Prévôté* in 1752.[24]

In the seventeenth century roofing materials were a secondary concern to the authorities. Wooden shingles were blamed for the spread of blazes that began as chimney fires, for where else did the flying sparks settle other than on roofs? The *Conseil souverain* boldly outlawed the use of wooden shingles within the towns in 1688.[25] A year later the council retreated and it sanctioned the use of oak and walnut (*noyer*) shingles on dormers.[26] This was ineffective; cedar shingles continued to be used because that wood was easy to split and it resisted decay. In 1706 the *Conseil supérieur* admitted that the houses of Quebec's Lower Town "are all roofed with wood shingles"[27] and cedar shingles were still a common form of roofing in the towns in 1727.[28] Townspeople were not content with the plain board roofs of the countryside and they could not afford tiles or slate for roofing. These would have had to come from France and, moreover, tiles could not endure the combination of moisture and frost in Eastern Canada. Slate and tin leaf roofs could, however, be seen on public and church buildings in the colony.

In 1721 the authorities in New France were jolted into action and their half-hearted attacks against the use of wooden shingles in the towns became a vigorous crusade against all wooden structures in Montreal and Quebec. The event that brought about this transformation occurred at Montreal, a town nearly as large as Quebec. During a Corpus Christi procession in June, a musketeer, who was among those firing a salute, carelessly discharged his weapon in the direction of the chapel of the Hôtel-Dieu. The roof caught fire and when the conflagration had exhausted itself, 138 buildings had been completely or partially destroyed. Nearly half had been built of stone, but most had been roofed with cedar shingles.[29] In his report to the intendant, the King's Engineer attributed the disaster to the wooden houses and said, in spite of the evidence, "that most of the said houses were only built of wood or *colombage* and supported a roof frame of heavy timber, which spread this fire."[30]

On the basis of this report, Intendant Michel Bégon decreed in July,

1721, that, in future, houses built in Montreal would be "of stone and two storeys high, the ground floor included, with a roof resting on purlins or gutter boards." The point in having the roof underlaid with purlins (*filières*) or longtitudinal strips of wood was, that being thus loosely attached to the rafters, the roof covering could be easily wrenched off in a fire. Roofs henceforth would receive a double covering of boards "until it is possible to use tiles or slate." Mansard roofs, which had been fashionable in late seventeenth century Quebec, were also outlawed because of the mass of combustible framing involved, and attic floors were to be overlaid with a fireproof layer of flagstones or brick on a bed of three or four *pouces* of mortar. Montrealers were allowed three years of grace for full compliance with this law[31] and, in fact, many went on building their houses as they had done before.

Bégon's building *ordonnance* of 1721 was a precedent for a comprehensive building code for all the towns of the St. Lawrence valley. The new code was issued by Intendant Claude-Thomas Dupuy on June 7th, 1727, and it incorporated the ideas of the King's Engineer, Gaspard-Joseph Chaussegros de Léry, as well as the principles of previous legislation. This lengthy ordinance restated, with some minor variations, the earlier regulations on alignments, projections, chimneys, fireproof attic floors, stone gables above the roof line, mansard roofs and roofing materials. Frame houses, whether of *pièces-sur-pièces* or *colombage*, were forbidden "even if they were built with the intention of covering them with a lime and sand plaster." "A material as pernicious as the cedar shingles used in this country" was provisionally tolerated for rural dwellings alone. This code, with its 21 articles, was not only more detailed than any body of regulations issued before, it also ventured into new areas of house construction hitherto ignored by the magistracy. In so doing, the law entertained a new consideration beyond symmetry, sanitation and the danger of fire.

The code of 1727 stipulated that, without a cellar, urban houses would be two storeys high and that, with a cellar, the main floor would have to be 12 *pieds* high. Moreover, half of the cellar was to be below ground level. Buildings meeting these requirements would make better use of the land within the towns. In a masonry wall there were to be no structural members of wood, such as lintels. All openings were to be framed in stone. Floor joists were to be framed around hearths (*enchevêtrure de bois*) and not pass under them. This was clearly to prevent fires. Roof trusses were to be an equilateral triangle based on the width of the house to allow sweeps and firefighters to mount the slope. A roof slope of 60 degrees was already accepted in the eighteenth century and fashion would have seen to the observance of this rule, as long as mansards were forbidden. The novel

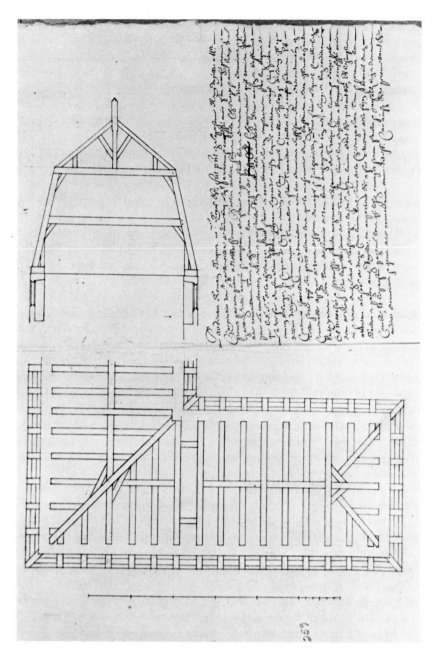

Plan for a high mansard roof (1679).

58

consideration in all of this is revealed by article 3 that dealt with cellars. Cellars were to be vaulted and at least six *pieds* deep "to prevent decay in the beams and floors placed above them, which in rotting would sooner or later become a fatal hazard to those occupying the house."[32] The new principle contained in this code was that construction be durable and safe.

The 1727 ordinance was sufficiently comprehensive to require little supplementary legislation. The code applied to private dwellings in towns and in the 1750s the people of Trois-Rivières and Montreal were told that the interdict on wooden houses also extended to timber outbuildings.[33] A fire at Quebec in the spring of 1754 led to an additional ordinance enacted by Intendant François Bigot that fixed the height of fire gables in that town at three *pieds* above the roof level with projecting stone corbels (*accoyaux*) where the eave extended beyond the wall face.[34] Those familiar with traditional, urban architecture in the Province of Quebec will at once recognize in these laws the origin of many of the stylistic features such as the heavy fire gables with parapet walls and the massive chimneys rising well above the roofs.

When compared with construction in wood, masonry buildings differed in more than complexity and cost. Without doubt, stone dwellings were costly and they required the services of a variety of craftsmen and labourers. Stone houses were also built for a different clientele and this had an effect on the building procedure. In the seventeenth century most clients were preoccupied with economy, and they did as much as they could for themselves. This was particularly true of the rural *habitants* contracting for a wooden building. Even in the masonry contracts made before 1700, two out of every three patrons assumed the responsibility of supplying the building materials, with the exception of the dressed stonework. Between 1700 and 1735 the parties to an agreement for a stone house took on that responsibility equally. After 1735 most customers were content to leave the problem of the building materials in the hands of the masonry contractor. This trend was a reflection of the times and of the wealth of the clients. In the countryside during the eighteenth century there were a number of farmers who could afford a stone house; in the towns the patrons of masonry builders were more likely to be merchants and public officials. Building in stone required substantial credit and personal wealth; the cost discouraged those of modest fortune. In 1730 a Quebec shoemaker who had paid an advance on the construction of a *pièces-sur-pièces* house in the town demanded his money back from the builder when he realized that the law would not permit a wooden house to be built. There was no point in changing the specifications for the material for, as the shoemaker told the intendant, he could only afford a wooden house.[35] Cost was the principal difference between building in wood and building in stone. A *pièces-sur-pièces* cottage could be erected for less than 300 *livres* whereas the cost of a stone building began at around 450 *livres* and it easily attained 2,000 or more *livres*. It was not a home for a poor man.

In agreements for frame houses the carpenter promised delivery of the completed shell with floor joists and a roof frame for a fixed price of, say, 50 to 300 *livres*. This was called a *marché en bloc*. It was almost unheard of to have a builder work for a daily wage paid by the client.[36] The fixed price contract or *marché en bloc* was very common in masonry contracts of the seventeenth century, and it was customary when building just a chimney. In the eighteenth century the masonry builder assumed a greater responsibility, not only for the construction materials, but also for the entire house, including roof covering, flooring, joinery and ironwork. The stonemason had become a builder-contractor and he employed, in turn, workers in other crafts as his subcontractors. The building contractors of New France usually came from the ranks of the stonemasons, who had experience in subcontracting; very few contractors came from other trades, and only one, to my knowledge, was a woman.[37] A contract for an entire house ready for occupancy was termed *marché les clefs à la main*, for the client received the keys to a finished home. The builder in this case was an entrepreneur, for he was gambling that he could provide a variety of materials and services for an agreed price with something extra as his profit. There were too many variables of supply and cost to permit one to predict the total cost of a house with absolute certainty. Because of the costs involved in hiring a work force, subcontracting with other artisans, and in dealing with wood and stone suppliers, the "contractor" was frequently two masonry builders in partnership. Few individual masons had the resources to undertake a *marché les clefs à la main* for a large stone house.

Rather than mislead the reader into thinking that, at last, we have discovered evidence in the masonry contracts of the commercial entrepreneurship that was said to be wanting among *Canadiens* of the French regime, it should be noted that in the eighteenth century the risk was removed from these ventures by a simple expedient. The expedient was payment *à la toise*. This meant that the builder was paid a set price for every cubic *toise* or fathom of masonry wall. This would be rubble-stone masonry and it was customarily measured, under the *Coûtume de Paris*, "tant plein que vide." That is to say, it was all measured as though it were solid wall, without any reduction for openings. A separate price was set for the dressed stone around the openings and it was paid for by the linear *pied* or at so many *livres* per window or door. This stonework was more expensive than rubble wall because it took a great deal of labour to cut and dress stone.

The caution of clients and builders in New France is revealed by their growing preference for masonry contracts payable by piecework or *à la toise*. Before 1700 only a third of the contracts seen used this form of payment. In the next 35 years the proportions were reversed: only a third of the accords were *en bloc*. In the last 25 years of the French regime, the two types of contract were almost balanced and that was because of the increase in *marchés les clefs à la main*. It was the age of wealthy patrons and large-scale contractors, many of whom had made their fortunes in building fortifications for the Crown. By their number and nature, the contracts for masonry buildings mirrored the colony's prosperity in the mid-eighteenth century.

In the eighteenth century we are not only dealing with a wealthier population, but we are also talking about bigger houses. With wooden structures, it was a matter of a few feet added to the length and breadth of the house. Stone dwellings of the period were commonly 30 to 40 *pieds* long and 20 to 25 *pieds* wide. They could be larger in area and they were more likely to be two storeys high than wooden houses. They invariably had a cellar.

The same canny prudence evident in the growing preference for contracts *à la toise* showed itself in the time chosen for drawing up an accord for a stone house. Many seventeenth century clients dallied until late winter before making arrangements with a builder. In time, more and more saw the wisdom, so evident in the carpentry contracts, of tying down the contractor well in advance of the following construction season. In the 1700s just over half went to the notary in the autumn to conclude the agreement with the builder. The intervening winter was then employed in making subcontracts with workmen and suppliers so that all would be ready for a quick start "dès le petit printemps prochain," as the *Canadiens* were accustomed to saying.[38]

This foresight was forced on the colonists by the climate of the St. Lawrence valley. Lime mortar cures slowly and, in a frost, it will be broken up by the expanding water crystals. At Quebec the mean temperature is above the freezing point from the end of March to mid-November. Rain is another factor, for it will wash away fresh mortar, not to speak of the discomfort of the mason. Masonry work is, therefore, further confined by the need for dry and warm days. Precipitation in the Quebec region drops off sharply after April and it resumes at a high level in November.[39] Climate imposes a severe restraint on masonry construction in that area now and the winters of the French regime may have been more severe, for the administrators claimed that masonry work then could only be accomplished during five months of the year, rather than the seven as indicated above. "It is true," wrote the governor and the intendant in 1693, "that workers' wages here are high, but at the same time it must be remembered that, because of the rigour of the winter, these men can only work for five months of the year, and in this time they have to earn enough to survive in the seven other months."[40]

The building of a stone house in Eastern Canada was a race against the winter. Clients were often insistent that the builder start in the early spring, "as soon as spring begins and the snow has melted" in the words of one contract.[41] The usual requirement was that the builder begin work just as soon as the weather permitted and, at the latest, by May 15th. The masonry walls and gables were to be ready to receive the woodwork by late June or early July and the house was to be roofed and complete by late September or, at least, in November. The winter weather would have done havoc to unprotected stonework. November 1st, All Saints' Day, was a popular terminal date, for it was then that indentured masonry workers were usually laid off. The choice of religious feast-days to mark off the completion of different stages of the project was a well-used practice. The feast of St. John the Baptist (June 24th), St. Martin's Day (Sept. 29th), and All Saints' Day were popular choices. These were convenient landmarks whose selection was ultimately determined by the weather and, with it, agriculture. The feast of St. John the Baptist was the eve of haying when every hand was needed in the fields. Two Montrealers specified that construction would only begin after sowing.[42] The townsfolk of Quebec were not as subject to the dictates of agriculture. The interest behind the selection of a religious holiday is shown in a contract whose deadline was "by the end of next autumn as long as it is possible to do masonry work . . . , at least until the feast of All Saints' Day."[43]

We now have the typical building sequence for a stone house in New France: the contract was signed in the fall, the materials and site were prepared over the winter, the foundations were laid in late April or early May, the walls would be complete by about the end of June, the floor joists would be installed and the roof frame raised by July 15th, the floors and roof were covered in August, and the doors and windows were in place by November 1st. The pattern was variable: a minority of contracts permitted construction to begin in a season other than spring and a few allowed construction to extend over a year. The number of workers on the job and the size of the building to be completed affected the rate of progress. In the best of circumstances, a stone house could be built in three months. Carpenters were less hampered by the exigencies of the weather and they could begin work at an earlier date. One lightning woodworker promised in February to erect a frame house 36 *pieds* long, with a board roof "before the next sowing."[44]

NOTES

1. P.F.X. de Charlevoix, *Histoire et Description Generale*, V, 107.
2. A.J.H. Richardson, "A Comparative Historical Study of Timber Construction in Canada," *Bulletin of the Association for Preservation Technology*, V (1973): 3, 77-88.
3. G.M. Wrong (ed.), *Lettre d'un Habitant de Louisbourg, 1745* (Toronto, 1897), 26. Thomas Pichon, *Lettres et Memoires Pour Servir a l'Histoire Naturelle, Civile et Politique du Cap Breton* (The Hague, 1760), 9, says exactly the same thing.
4. A.N., A.C., Depôt des fortifications des Colonies (Amérique septentrionale), Mémoire No. 469 (Levasseur de Neré, 15 nov. 1704).
5. Antoine Roy (ed.), *L'Ile de Montréal en 1731* (Quebec, 1943), introduction.
6. O.C.G.I., I, 135. Servants in Quebec were still emptying chamber pots into the streets in 1750. See A.Q., N.F. 19 (Prévôté de Québec), XCV, ff. 10-10vo.
7. O.C.G.I., I, 192.
8. J.D.C.S., V, 237.
9. J.D.C.S., V, 336-7, 344-5.
10. A.Q., N.F. 19, LXXXVIII, ff. 5vo-6.
11. J.D.C.S., III, 329.
12. I.O.I., III, 171-2; A.Q., N.F. 23, XIII (Juridiction de Trois-Rivières), ff. 30.
13. J.D.C.S., I, 725, 753.
14. O.C.G.I., I, 137-8.
15. O.C.G.I., I, 137.
16. J.D.C.S., III, 206,
17. O.C.G.I., II, 174-8.
18. J.D.C.S., III, 206.
19. A.N., A.C., série C11A, LI, f.114.
20. E.O.R., II, 317.
21. Edouard-Zotique Massicotte, *Répertoire des arrêts, édits, mandements, ordonnances et règlements conservées dans les archives du Palais de justice de Montréal 1640-1760* (Montreal, 1919), 116-7.
22. A.Q.M., G.N.R.F., A. Adhémar, 22 avril 1689, 25 sept. 1692; J.C. Raimbault, 20 mars 1732; A.Q., G.N.R.F., C. Barolet, 20 mai 1755, 3 août 1755; J.C. Panet, 7 sept. 1757.
23. A.Q., N.F. 19, XCV, ff.5-6; N.F. 25 (Collection de pièces judiciaires et notariales), No. 1388 (Procès-verbal d'une visite générale de la ville de Québec pour l'inspection des cheminées, 11 mai 1744); P.A.C., M.G. 8, B 1, XX-1, 184-196 (juillet 1729).
24. A.Q., N.F. 19, XCV, ff.13-13vo.
25. J.D.C.S., III, 206.
26. J.D.C.S., III, 329.

27. J.D.C.S., V, 446.
28. A.Q., N.F. 2 (Ordonnances des intendants), XIIa, ff.138vo-140vo; E.O.R., II, 316. In 1796 Elizabeth Simcoe noted that at Quebec "the Churches and Houses" were "covered with singles." See Mary Q. Innis (ed.), *Mrs. Simcoe's Diary* (Toronto, 1971), 199.
29. E.Z. Massicotte, "L'Incendie du Vieux Montréal," *Bulletin des Recherches historiques*, XXXII (1926), 583-608.
30. *Ibid.*, 606.
31. E.O.R., II, 292-4.
32. E.O.R., II, 314-321.
33. I.O.I., III, 171-2; E.Z. Massicotte, *Répertoire*, 130-1.
34. E.O.R., II, 418; I.O.I., III, 186.
35. A.Q., N.F. 2, XVII, ff.100-100vo.
36. A.Q., G.N.R.F., L. Chambalon, 8 oct. 1710. This would be called a *marché à la journée*.
37. A.Q.M., G.N.R.F., C. Maugue, 13 nov. 1695 (Madeleine Chrestien, widow Chicouane, who undertook miscellaneous repairs and improvements on the house of Pierre Bienvenu and his wife).
38. This expression is used in A.Q., G.N.R.F., C. Barolet, 25 nov. 1752; F. Genaple, 29 nov. 1688; and elsewhere.
39. Georges Gauthier-Larouche, *Evolution de la maison rurale traditionnelle dans la région de Québec* (Québec, 1974), 61 (Sommaire climatique de la région de Québec).
40. P.A.C., C11A transcript, XII-2, 429-430.
41. A.Q., G.N.R.F., F. Genaple, 18 nov. 1682.
42. A.Q.M., G.N.R.F., B. Basset, 11 fév. 1665, 22 fév. 1666.
43. A.Q., G.N.R.F., F. Genaple, 2 déc. 1686.
44. A.Q.M., G.N.R.F., B. Basset, 11 fév. 1660.

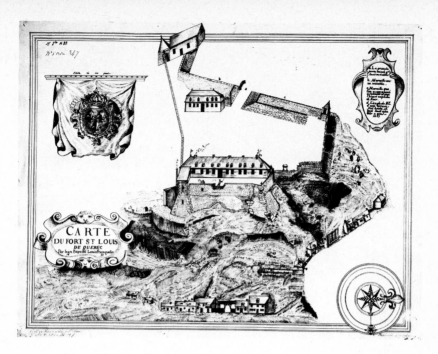

Franquelin's view of the governor's fortified mansion and adjacent buildings at Quebec in 1683 is a record of seventeenth century urban styles. The house at the fort gate has a mansard roof while those in the Lower Town are enlivened with dormers, suspended signs, exterior stairways and galleries.

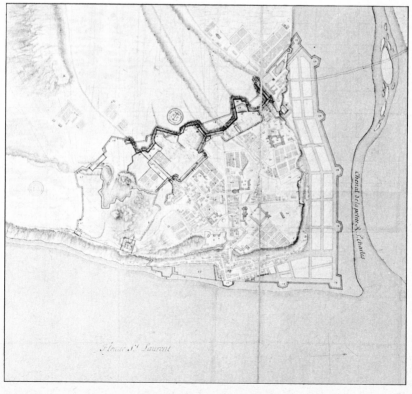

Map of Quebec City, 1709.

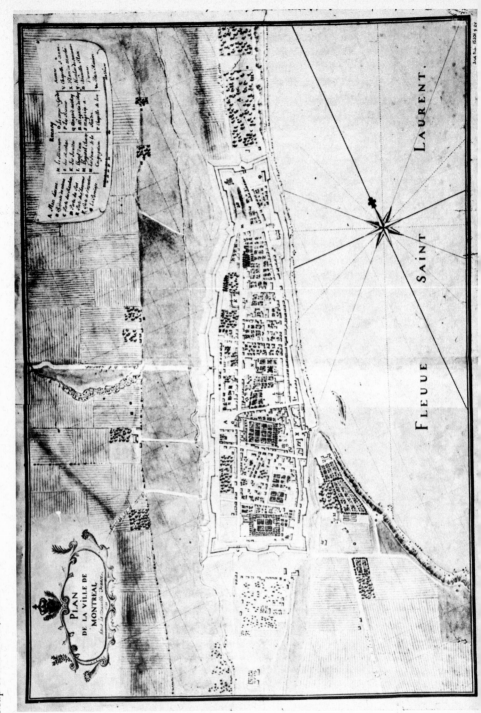

Map of Montreal, 1731.

66

This seventeenth century building at Sainte-Laurent-sur-Manoire in France is a fine example of the form and proportions that were reproduced in the first generation of houses in New France. The collapse of the centre of this structure has conveniently revealed the framing of the roof which, by Canadian standards, is fairly complex.

The hospital and quayside quarter, Louisbourg, 1731. This view shows the range of construction techniques used in that town. The hospital and public buildings are of masonry while the private houses nearby are half-timbered or have walls of framed *piquets*. Close to the quay, and presumably connected with the fishery, are huts of sod and of *piquets* planted in the ground. Such huts would also be found in the other French settlements of Cape Breton and Newfoundland.

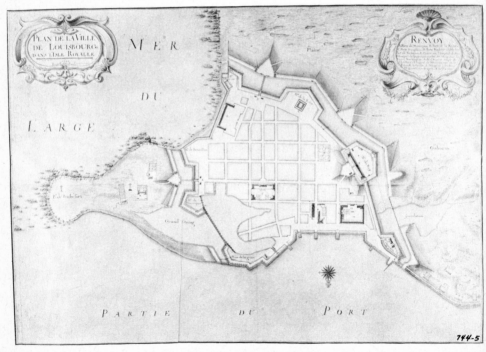

Map of Louisbourg, 1744.

"This scene of French tile roofers at work had only a few parallels with the roofer's trade in Canada; both the supporting lattice work and fragile materials such as tiles and slate were abandoned by private builders. Colonial roofers laid overlapping boards or shingles over a solid layer of boards. In the background a passer-by flees falling debris.''

The house-framer's work yard: in the foreground a hand axe is used to trim a beam, a worker with a chisel cuts a mortise and another smooths a shoulder with a long chisel. Pit sawyers labour in the background. A shed is available for shelter in bad weather. On the left is the incomplete frame of a half-timbered house.

The Genius of Architecture presiding over angelic stonemasons of a type not known in Canada, 1738.

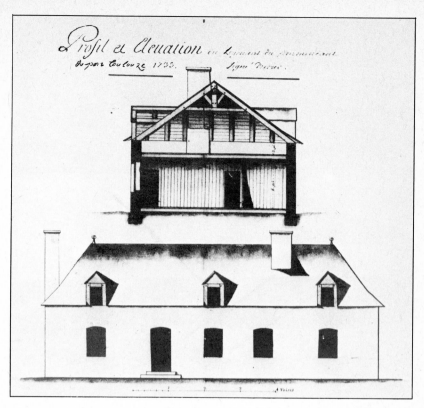

Etienne Verrier's 1733 plan and elevation of the military commander's house at Port Toulouse (St. Peter's N.S.) is one of the few illustrations we have of wooden partition walls and the primary layer of boards between the rafters and the roof covering.

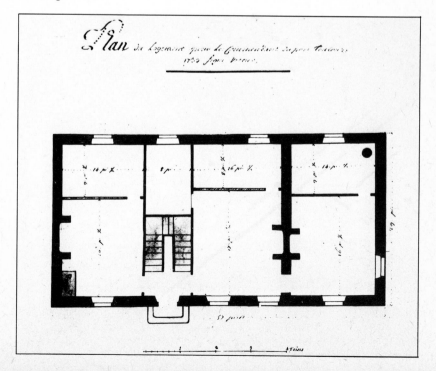

Thomas Davies' view of Château-Richer in 1787 shows the variety of roofing materials (boards, wood shingles, and thatch) and wall construction (frame, rubble-stone, and post in ground) used for farm buildings in the St. Lawrence valley.

Davies in 1789 found the *Place d'Armes* little changed since the 1750s. His drawing shows how whitewashed roughcasting was used to cover masonry walls, leaving only the cut stone margins of the windows and doors clear. Note also the board roofs and the shutters on the ground floor windows. Passers-by were evidently a greater hazard than weather.

4

A Tale Of Two Houses

In the Montreal notarial and judicial archives there is the melancholy history of a pair of adjoining houses built by two brothers in the eighteenth century. The brothers were Jean-Baptiste and Antoine-Bertrand, the sons of Antoine Forestier. They, like their father, were surgeons and their sister Elisabeth kept up the family tradition by marrying Joseph Istre, yet another surgeon. All three planned to live side by side on Notre-Dame street on land that originally belonged to their late father. Jean-Baptiste inherited his lot, while Antoine-Bertrand bought a 32½ *pieds* square section of his sister's inheritance in August, 1729.[1] The 1,600 *livres* given in payment was largely a five-year loan from Jean Boucher, called Belleville, a major contractor. Merchants were the usurers of New France, but this was an exception like that of the first Château de Ramezay, which was financed by the friendly, neighbourhood Franciscan friars.[2]

Jean-Baptiste Forestier seemed to have money of his own and, as soon as his father's estate was settled, he began to make plans for his house. His contractor was Jacques Dielle, a blacksmith who obviously felt that he could be as good an entrepreneur as any stonemason. Under their agreement of December, 1728, Dielle undertook the construction of a house "built of stone, whose dimensions will be just 37 *pieds* along Notre-Dame street, leaving a five *pieds* strip free beside the house for a passageway to the courtyard, and 35 *pieds* deep. The said house will be one storey high, consisting of the ground floor with an attic above it." The structure was to be erected on a foundation of two-and-a-half *pieds* above ground level with vents (*soupiraux*) "like those of Toussaint La Marche's house." On the street face there would be two doors with steps and three windows. Of the remaining five windows, four would be in the rear and one would be placed in the northeast wall. Dielle was to supply all the hardware, presumably of his own workmanship, including "a good, iron clamp for hanging a crane [for cooking pots]" in the kitchen hearth. The same room would also have a stone wash-basin set in the ledge of a rear window. Inset cupboards were comprised in the joinery-work along with an unusual ground floor of "bearing joists . . . furrowed (*cannelé*) to support a primary floor of cedar [posts] with lime mortar caulking in all the joints and a layer of earth one *pouce* . . . above the thickest post." The object of this strange floor of cedar posts covered with earth must have been insulation from the cold. The boards on the roof were explicitly to have a four *pouces* overlap. The price for the entire house was 2,500 *livres* payable in wheat over the winter, beaver pelts in the summer and the balance in goods at retail value. Jean-Baptiste's secondary role as fur trader[3] made this a convenient form of payment. For this sum Dielle would deliver the house to Forestier "Les Clefs a La main." If he could not finish the home in 1729 he promised that he would have half of it ready for occupancy "on All Saints' Day at the latest."[4]

The details provided by the Forestier-Dielle contract are sufficient to allow one to reconstruct the outward appearance of the house and this has been done in the accompanying sketch. The deed also leaves no doubt about the floor plan of the completed building because the amended plan is still with the contract. This is a stroke of good fortune. The structure was to be built "according to the drawing and plan made for it and now signed and initialed by the said parties and notaries." The procedure of having a general plan that was co-signed with the contract was not unusual; the plan would then, as a rule, be handed over to the builder. Since these drawings had no legal value after the house was completed and accepted, they were never retrieved from the contractor. As a consequence, very few plans for private dwellings in New France exist. They probably were discarded or lost by the builder and the historical researcher is condemned to the frustration of reading contracts that refer him to a plan that is no longer there. The few drawings that have survived owe their existence to a happy accident: the original was traced on the contract and then copied for the craftsman.[5] Elevations for the construction of a private house are the ultimate rarity and the one reproduced here has been worked up from a fragment of the drawing that was used by the builder to write a message to a notary.[6] Such are the fortunes of survival.

Many plans and elevations were likely torn up for scrap paper and we may thank heaven for the decision in December, 1728, to deviate from the usual procedure of surrendering the plan to the contractor. The floor plan of the Jean-Baptiste Forestier home was filed with the building contract to be "exhibited for the inspection of the work done." What we have, however, is not the first floor plan; it is an amended drawing of the interior showing changes agreed to by the parties in 1729. The signature on the plan throws light on those who served as architectural draughtsmen for private clients, for the author of this drawing was Paul Jourdain La Brosse, a Montreal sculptor and joiner. The revised floor plan, reproduced here with notations, shows the location of the hearths, inset cupboards, partition walls and even the proverbial kitchen sink. It also reveals the more complex subdivision of space in urban dwellings into vestibule, study, kitchen and so on. *Tambour* was the term used for an inside vestibule or an exterior enclosure for the main door and both prevented wintry gusts from accompanying anyone who entered the house.

Front elevation of the possible appearance of the Forestier House on Notre-Dame St., using the specifications given in the Dec. 20, 1728, building contract drawn up by the notary, Guillet de Chaumont.

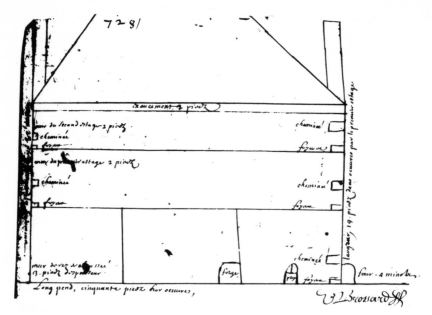

A crudely-drawn plan for a large, general-purpose building at Fort Lachine (1672).

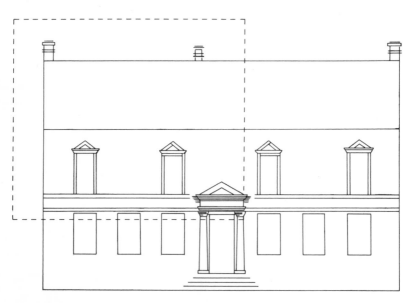

Elevation of a house (c. 1700), reconstructed from a fragment of a drawing by François De Lajoue, Quebec architect.

Dielle's first task in April, 1729, was to level the house already on Jean-Baptiste Forestier's land and to clear the building site. This was ordinarily the duty of the client and the builder of the Louis Jolliet house at Quebec was given a special payment "to clear the building site."[7] Builders could be induced to accept the responsibility for demolition in return for salvage rights to the old building. Dielle accepted this arrangement with the proviso that he not use the salvaged lumber for the partition walls of the new house. Appearance was important, and scarred and stained boards would do little for the reputation of the surgeon. Forestier's offer was generous for, in similar circumstances, clients liked to reserve the ironwork, bricks, dressed stone and a few choice beams for themselves before abandoning the rest to the wrecker.[8] Salvaged materials could be discreetly incorporated into the new building, which was a saving for the contractor who was bound to supply his own construction materials. At Quebec it was common practice to reuse old masonry as wall fill and as interior facing, which would then be plastered over. Old foundations that were judged fit to support the new structure were retained as a further economy; this is what was done in this case. The Forestier house was built over the cellar of its predecessor and Dielle lined the interior of the cellar with roughcasting which concealed the fact that it was old stonework. He was also directed to level the old walls down to the street level on the front and "down to the foundations" at the rear. There is no reference to salvaging stonework, and so the upper walls of the older building must have been made of wood. Throughout this you will note that Forestier saved what he could of the previous dwelling while having these economies concealed with the appearance of new construction, particularly on the street face.

By August, 1729, the masonry house on Notre-Dame street was well under way. We know this because on the 10th of the month Jean-Baptiste Forestier sold his brother-in-law, Joseph Istre, the right to use the southwest side as a common wall. Istre paid 80 *livres* for half of the land on which it stood and he agreed to share the cost of its construction.[9] This windfall allowed Forestier to think on a grander scale. A few days later Dielle acknowledged receipt of 2,510 *livres*, 11 *sols* to date and, for an extra 400 *livres*, he consented to add a central hearth that was not provided for in the original contract. This was when La Brosse drew up the revised plan.[10]

The woodwork of Forestier's house was not finished in the first year of construction. In March, 1730, Jacques Cusson, a joiner, subcontracted with Dielle to complete the woodwork inside the house. The departure of the previous joiner or carpenter was not explained. For 100 *livres* and the metalwork of a large bed "ala mode," Cusson undertook "to finish the

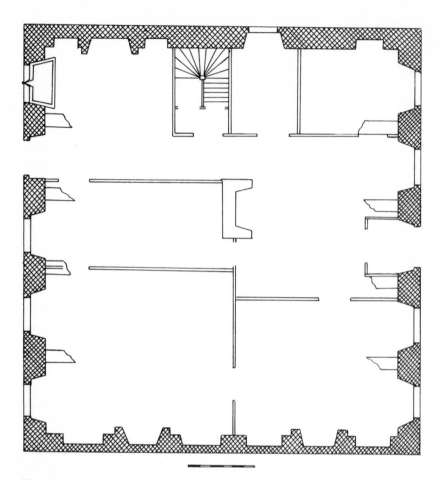

Floor plan of a one-storey stone house designed for Jean-Baptiste Forestier, Montréal surgeon, and to be built by Jacques Dielle, entrepreneur and blacksmith. The architect was, apparently, Paul Jourdain LaBrosse, surveyor and sculptor.

upper and lower floors, install two panelled doors and seven [batten] doors with dovetailed cross-bars, the partition walls, and a stairway . . . following the plan," of which he was given a copy.[11] For the sake of appearance, the front doors were "divided into raised panels (*brisés a panneaux couverts*) with three hinges on each one." The hinges on the doors, cupboards and windows and the sliding bolts to secure them would come from Dielle's forge. It is certain that he hired a mason and a roofer, though no notarized contracts for their work exist. The agreement could have been verbal or, more likely, it was a holograph (*sous seing privé*) contract drawn

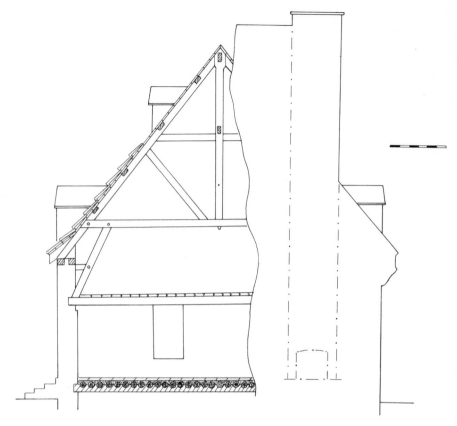

Cross section from the northeast of the J.-B. Forestier House. Stone gable wall
cut away to expose structure.

up by the contractor and signed by the parties. The unregistered accords
were brief and to the point. One reads: "I, that is me Charles Viollet, bind
myself to roof the new house of Madame Poinsu with shingles and to
supply all the shingles and nails required for the sum of 150 *livres*, that the
said lady will pay me on St. Michael's Day next."[12] When finished, the
roof of the Forestier house was to have five dormer windows and the
roofer would be paid something extra for covering these in addition to the
roof proper.

When Jacques Dielle received the final payment of some 390 *livres* in
June, 1732, the house was described as being "built . . . following and in
keeping with the specifications and contract."[13] The total cost of the building, materials included had come to 2,900 *livres*, but part of this was paid
by Joseph Istre.

On the very day in 1729 when Istre contracted to share the cost of one gabled-wall of Jean-Baptiste's house, Antoine-Bertrand Forestier bought the lot next door. He had decided to emulate his brother and the fact that part of Jean-Baptiste's house had been subsidized by a neighbour may have given Antoine *fils* hopes of similar assistance. The brothers were both surgeons, it is true, but Antoine lacked the resources of Jean-Baptiste, who was also engaged in the fur trade. The fact that Antoine had bought his building lot with borrowed money was proof of this. He also tried to "cut corners" by acting as his own general contractor and the result was a fiasco.

Before setting out for Quebec in the summer of 1729, Antoine gave his power of attorney to his wife, Elisabeth Camoint, so that she could negotiate with the craftsmen. Her first contract was made in September with Toussaint Périneau, called Lamarche, a Montreal mason. He bound himself to execute "all of the said masonry work with good quarry stone, as is required for a house ... of the length and breadth that the said Sieur Forestier judges suitable, and according to the plan and the drawing which will be given to him [Lamarche]. He is to plaster over the joints (*renduire ... a joint*) on the outside of the walls and in the attic to the top of the chimneys and gable. And on the inside [of the ground floor] he will cover the entire wall with roughcasting and then plaster ... which he will whitewash." Plastering over the joints between stones on the exterior protected the bonding mortar and it gave the wall a more finished appearance. Roughcasting was sometimes applied over the entire surface and it provided a smooth finish in a colony where few could afford the luxury of a dressed stone facade. In private homes cut stone, as a rule, was used solely for window and door margins, exterior corners, decorative string courses and, inside, for framing fireplaces. Smooth dressing with a chisel (*pierre taillée au cizeau*) was an extravagance reserved for the main entrance and the principal, downstairs hearth. Stone roughly dressed with a mason's point (*piquée*) was cheaper and it was used elsewhere in the house. All of the stonework in Jean-Baptiste's home was rough-dressed with the exception of the sink and some moulding around the kitchen fireplace. The interior finish of plaster (*enduit*) over roughcasting (*crépi*) made of sand and lime, with a final covering of whitewash, was a common feature in early French-Canadian houses.

This contract with the mason betrays the impatience, confusion and poverty of Antoine Forestier and his wife. They did not have, as yet, plans for their house nor had they even decided on its dimensions. Périneau Lamarche was going to be paid *à la toise* 14 *livres* and ten *sols* for the masonry walls and, "for each of the said [dressed stone] windows, doors, chimneys and hearths" 15 *livres*. The price was in order since the mason would be supplying his own stone, sand and lime as well as any helpers and scaffolding he might need. Had he furnished his labour alone, the price per *toise* of wall would have been just five or six *livres*.[14]

Antoine and his wife Elisabeth may have thought themselves more shrewd than Jean-Baptiste by making a *marché à la toise*. They also decided that they would "have the excavations necessary for the said wall foundations done themselves." This was popular wisdom; why pay a skilled tradesman to do unskilled work? A day labourer was usually engaged by the client to dig the hole for the foundations or the cellar for

A cut stone fireplace was a refinement reserved for the principal downstairs room, when a client could afford such work.

wages or for so many *livres* per cubic *toise* of soil removed. It was an arrangement that was rarely committed to a notarized contract. A simple foundation, like the one in question, might require a trench three *pieds* deep.[15] In a 1714 *marché* a Quebec labourer agreed "to dig a hole on the lot . . . 20 *pieds* square . . . and 10 *pieds* deep below ground . . . , and to remove therefrom all the soil and stones" for sixty *livres*. As for the disposal of the dirt, the worker proposed "to throw the earth onto the streets passing the said site" with the customer's blessing.[16] This was cheaper than paying a carter to haul it away in a tumbrel. What the neighbours or the authorities thought of this method of disposal can be imagined.

The masonry contract was not made until late September and the Forestiers still expected to begin work that year. Périneau Lamarche was told to hold himself in readiness to start work " at the first call to be made upon him, so that he will have the foundations built up to the level of the ground floor in this year, and when next spring comes (*des Le Petit Printemps prochain*) he will resume and continue the said work without a break until its completion" so that the roof could be framed in July. Payment for his work would be made in grain, letters of credit or currency, and in goods. The clients hoped to reduce the cost by supplying some of the labour and materials themselves, for which the mason was obliged to give them credit.[17]

Mme. Forestier's next contract was concluded in October, 1729, with Jean-Baptiste Le Cavelier, called Rangeard, a local joiner. Rangeard was qualified to be a house-framer for he agreed to produce "the frame (*charpente*), beams, joists, sleepers, dormers and primary floors of cedar posts, . . . whether for the cellar or for the attic . . . , and the roof frame as soon as the walls are ready to receive it" for 260 *livres* in miscellaneous goods. This was not a proper joinery contract since it did not mention partitions, cupboards, doors, windows or shutters, and no house would be complete without them. Perhaps, the Forestiers planned to defer that expense until a later date. At least by October they had decided on the dimensions of their future home; according to this contract, the house was to be 27 *pieds* along the street and 35 *pieds* in depth.[18] The 1731 *aveu et denombrement* for Montreal Island added that it was a one storey building with a yard and garden.[19]

Since Rangeard was to supply his own lumber, it is surprising to find Mme. Forestier contracting with an *habitant* of Longue Pointe in late October to have 250 pine planks (*madriers*) delivered to the building site by the end of April. The planks were to be ten *pieds* long, one *pied* wide and two *pouces* thick. Their thickness suggests that they were intended for flooring rather than for roofing. The price was set at 60 *livres* per hundred planks – boards being ordinarily sold by the hundred and beams being priced individually. Payment would be made "in goods from his [Forestier's] storehouse" and in roofing and flooring nails valued at three-and-a-half and two *livres* per hundred respectively.[20]

In the eighteenth century country folk used their free time over winter to cut and dress timber as well as to gather firewood for sale in the towns. In this period wood would be cut into boards at a water-powered sawmill and not be sawn by hand as before. The production of millwork was faster and cheaper than pit sawing and in eighteenth century Canada sawyers nearly disappeared as a specialized occupation. Wood supply contracts were generally more complex than this one and the *habitants* could furnish heavy planks (*madriers*), thin boards (*planches*), partition boards, joists (*lambourdes*), sills (*soles*) and beams (*poutres*). The individuality of the agreements would be in the lengths and in the types of wood desired.[21]

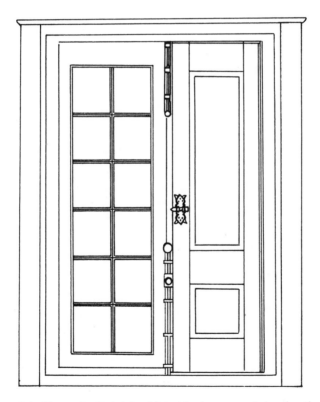

Window of the Ferme St. Gabriel, with inside shutters and showing the vertical sliding bolts to close the casements.

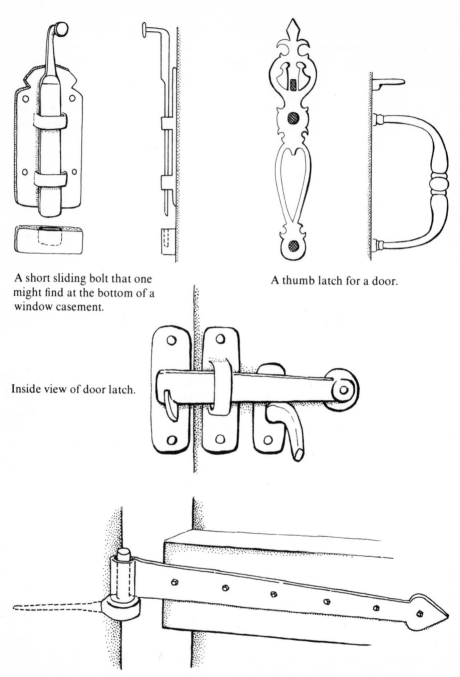

A short sliding bolt that one might find at the bottom of a window casement.

A thumb latch for a door.

Inside view of door latch.

Pintle and strap hinge, commonly used for hanging shutters, gates and heavy doors.

No locksmith's contract for the hardware of Antoine Forestier's house has been found; this may be another case of putting off what they could not yet afford or, at least, find credit for. On the other hand, acquisition of the ironwork could not be put off indefinitely and in New France an unlocked door was an invitation to theft. The Forestiers could not salvage the ironwork from their previous dwelling since, at that time, they were tenants in a rented house on Saint-François street. Judging from the debts for various unnamed goods that they had, it is probable that the Forestiers acquired their hardware ready-made from a local merchant.

The range of domestic hardware that would be found in such a house can be seen in a contract made for the nearby home of their brother-in-law Joseph Istre. In the winter of 1730-31 Istre listed the ironwork he required from a blacksmith-locksmith. Each casement window sash (*panneau*) would have two hinges (*fiches*) and a vertical, sliding bolt (*targette*). The window and door frames were to be secured by pins (*pattes*) set in the stonework. The exterior doors, front and back, were to be hung "with two hinges and two pins for each leaf (*panneaus*)" and secured by large, vertical spring-bolts (*targettes à ressort*). The transom above the back door, called "Le Chasy dessu la Porte," was likewise secured. This door was to be opened by a thumb-latch (*loquet à poignée*) and locked by a small cross-bolt (*verrou*) in addition to the spring-bolts. The main door had a large ring-latch (*loquet à boucle*) and key-operated lock. The cellar door and the passageway gate were to be hung on iron pintles (*gonds*) and be furnished with strap hinges (*pentures*). The blacksmith-locksmith promised similar hardware for two cupboards flanking the fireplace and pintles, hinges and hooks for the shutters at a total cost of 190 *livres*.[22]

The Forestiers were up to their necks in debt to the merchants of Montreal and all, it appears, for the sake of their house. Recall that they had borrowed 1,480 *livres* from Jean Boucher to pay for the building lot and that debt was due to be repaid in 1734.[23] They made out two more acknowledgements of debt (*actes d'obligation*). One was made in March, 1730, to Jacques and Louis Charly Saint-Ange, to whom the couple owed 3,600 *livres* "for goods supplied to them to be used in the building of the house that they are having constructed on Notre-Dame street in this town."[24] In April, 1732, the surgeon acknowledged another debt of 600 *livres* to François Montfort and Company "for fine and good merchandise sold and delivered to them [Forestier and his wife] for use in the building of a house . . . on Notre Dame street and for other needs."[25] In January of that year another merchant, Simon Réaume, and his wife had been awarded an unstated amount against Forestier by the *Conseil supérieur* of Quebec.[26] Antoine Forestier and Elisabeth Camoint owed over 6,000 *livres*; so much for their economies!

The couple had very little time in which to enjoy their new house. Forestier struggled to meet his obligations by pursuing patients in the Montreal court for small debts. In 1735 he and his wife were dispossessed by their own creditors. At the request of Jean Boucher, called Belleville, who claimed that they had incurred a debt of 2,800 *livres* and had only paid back a fraction of it, the house and lot were seized by a court order. At a judicial auction in September, 1735, the property was awarded to one Sieur Marin for a bid of 5,500 *livres*. Before Belleville could lay hold of all that was due him, five other creditors of Forestier intervened and demanded repayment of their accounts. The royal court at Montreal considered the conflicting demands and granted 2,500 *livres* each to Belleville and Louis Charly, as the principal creditors of the unfortunate and impetuous surgeon and his wife.[27]

NOTES

1. A.Q.M., G.N.R.F., J.C. Raimbault, 10 août 1729. For information on their father's estate, see *loc. cit.*, J.B. Adhémar, 2 déc. 1728.
2. A.Q.M., G.N.R.F., A. Adhémar, 19 juin 1706. Philippe de Rigaud was the secular intermediary through whom the Franciscans loaned 3,400 *livres* to Claude de Ramezay to pay his builder.
3. E.Z. Massicotte, "Congés et Permis déposés ou enregistrés à Montréal sous le régime français, " *R.A.P.Q.* 1921-1922, 219.
4. A.Q.M., G.N.R.F., N.A. Guillet de Chaumont, 20 déc. 1728.
5. A.N., A.C., série G3 (Notariat de Louisbourg), carton 2041-1, 6 oct. 1752; A.Q.M., G.N.R.F., B Basset, 22 fév. 1672; A.Q., G.N.R.F., R. Becquet, 3 mai 1679 (plasterwork for a fireplace).
6. A.Q., G.N.R.F., L. Chambalon, 17 fév. 1702.
7. Archives du Séminaire de Québec, Lettres Z, No. 9 (copy of a contract and *dévis* made on Dec. 1, 1683 and now in the possession of the Chicago Historical Society).
8. A.Q., G.N.R.F., F. Genaple, 22 avril, 14 jan. 1700; J.C. Panet, 7 Sept. 1757. The contractor who undertook the rebuilding of the Château Saint-Louis at Quebec in 1700 must have been pleased when he was told that he "pourra se servir des vieux materiaux quil trouvera propre a garnir le dedans desd[its] murs, et en prendra et enlevera au surplus a son profit particulier toute la vieille Charpente planchers et menuiseries, excepté les serrures." See A.Q., G.N.R.F., F. Genaple, 14 jan. 1700.
9. A.Q.M., G.N.R.F., N.A. Guillet de Chaumont, 10 août 1729.
10. Appendix of August 13, 1729 to the building contract cited in 4.
11. A.Q.M., G.N.R.F., J.C. Raimbault, 13 mars 1730.
12. A.N., A.C., série G2, CCIII (Bailliage de Louisbourg), dossier 301 (Poinsu estate, 5 nov. 1753).
13. Appendix of June 8, 1732 to the building contract cited in 4.

14. A.Q.M., G.N.R.F., N.A. Guillet de Chaumont, 24 jan. 1729; A.Q., G.N.R.F., J.E. Dubreuil, 29 oct. 1720, 21 avril 1722, 29 fév. 1728, 18 oct. 1728, 28 déc. 1730.
15. A.Q., G.N.R.F., F. Genaple, 17 déc. 1688.
16. A.Q., G.N.R.F., L. Chambalon, 19 avril 1714.
17. A.Q.M., G.N.R.F., J.C. Raimbault, 21 sept. 1729.
18. A.Q.M., G.N.R.F., J.C. Raimbault, 6 oct. 1729.
19. A. Roy (ed.), *L'Ile de Montréal en 1731*, 38.
20. A.Q.M., G.N.R.F., J.C. Raimbault, 21 oct. 1729.
21. A.Q.M., G.N.R.F., F. Simonnet, 14 fév. 1745; Archives judiciaires de Trois-Rivières [hereafter A.J.T.R.], P. Rigault, 26 mars 1757; A.N., A.C., série G3 (Notariat de Louisbourg), carton 2041-1, No. 102 (28 Oct. 1751), No. 131 (1 oct. 1752); A.Q., G.N.R.F., C. Barolet, 14 nov. 1752.
22. A.Q.M., G.N.R.F., J.C. Raimbault, 10 fév. 1731 (holograph *dévis* written by Joseph Istre and signed by Bernard Trutteau; when this document was deposited with the notary it was witnessed by Jacques Dielle who also acted as a witness to Mme. Forestier's contract with Périneau Lamarche).
23. A.Q.M., G.N.R.F., J.C. Raimbault, 11 août 1729.
24. A.Q.M., G.N.R.F., J.C. Raimbault, 16 mar 1730.
25. A.Q.M., G.N.R.F., N.A. Guillet de Chaumont, 24 avril 1732.
26. A.Q., N.F. 25 (Collection de pièces judiciaires et notariales), No. 882 (1731); I.J.D.C.S., II, 260.
27. A.Q., N.F. 21, VI (Juridiction de Montréal), ff. 113-4; X, 1er & 8 oct. 1735; I.J.D.C.S., II, 315; III, 3, 34, 223-4.

5

The Merchant Builders

It is a persistent myth of the industrial era that workers in a craft economy always did their work with pride and affection and that the relationship of craftsman and client was close and sympathetic. In eighteenth century New France masonry construction was "big business" and it involved dozens of workers unknown to the client. The masonry contractors grew on institutional contracts and, especially, on Crown contracts for fortifications. Domestic houses became a sideline for the large builder. In Canada the large-scale contractor first appeared at Quebec in the late seventeenth century. The names that come readily to mind are Claude Baillif, Jean Le Rouge and François De Lajoue, the latter, a wholesale merchant and builder who was the embodiment of entrepreneurship. Their successors in the following century included the Maillou brothers, Joseph and Jean-Baptiste; Jean Boucher, called Belleville, and Guillaume Deguise, called Flamand. The other towns had to wait until the eighteenth century before they could produce contractors of the same stature. Montreal was the home of Pierre Couturier, Jean Deslandes called Champigny, Jean-Baptiste Deguire, called LaRose, Paul Tessier called Lavigne, Pierre and Dominique Janson, called La Palme. At Louisbourg David Bernard Muiron, builder of the King's Works, undertook private contracts and Michel Dubenca was a notable carpenter-contractor. It was indicative of the small scale of things at Trois-Rivières that its principal, general contractor was a carpenter, François Dufaux.

The new builder-contractors were not just distinguished by the size of their undertakings; they were skilled professionals with a knowledge of classical design and complex business transactions. An ability to draw measured plans on paper earned them the title of "architecte." For the traditional artisan-builder and his clients, memory and the houses of the neighbourhood provided their architectural models. We have seen examples of contracts in which the builder was directed to reproduce a form or detail of an existing structure. For the large masonry contractors, guidance in design came from books and engravings. Claude Baillif possessed "ten little books as follows: La Coûtume de Paris, Les Récréations de Mathématiques, Chevalier de Ville's Fortifications, Savanne's Arithmétique, another copy of Les Récréations de Mathématiques, . . . [copies of] l'Architecture Françoise, La Règle des Cinq Corps (sic) d'Architecture by Vignola, another similar work by the same author, an abridgement of the Coûtume de Paris[1]". Here we recognize two standard references of French builders: Vignola's *Règles des cinq ordres d'architecture* and *L'Architecture françoise des bastimens particuliers* of Louis Savot. François Blondel, who edited later editions of *L'Architecture françoise*, said that Savot had written the book because "he had been distressed at seeing the ill-usage daily suffered by those who were obliged to pass through the hands of certain workers who were guilty of either ignorance or malice."[2] Blondel also described Vignola's work as "the first that students of architecture should read . . . It is also the best known book among workers."[3] The same two texts were to be found in the library of the Maillou brothers, former employees of Baillif who, as builders, enjoyed the patronage of the merchants and officials of Quebec as well as that of church and Crown. They also had copies of Vitruvius' *Architecture, ou art de bien bastir* and Philibert Delorme's *Le premier tome de l'architecture*, as well as 17 architectural engravings and two books on fortifications.[4] We are not so well informed on the handbooks used by the Montreal contractors. The Quebec Seminary does possess two volumes signed by Dominique Janson, called La Palme, who designed a number of churches in the Montreal region. The books are Augustin-Charles Davilier's *L'Architecture de Vignole* (Paris, 1720) and *Explication des termes d'architecture* (Paris, 1720). It should be noted that at this time architecture meant construction in stone, and carpentry was only considered worthy of study when it involved roof frames for masonry buildings.

The influence of architectural handbooks and experience with Crown contracts, whose specifications were prepared by military engineers, showed itself in the contracts draughted by the contractors for large stone dwellings. Quite apart from the contract itself, a *devis des ouvrages*, or statement of work to be done, was drawn up and in it the specifications for each aspect of the building were detailed. Here, for example, are some extracts from a 1737 *devis* for a home of two merchants at Louisbourg:[5]

Specifications for the work, whether masonry, carpentry, roofing, joinery, fittings and heavy ironwork, glazing, earthwork and paving, that he [the builder] agrees to do . . .

3^0

All of the mortar that will be used in the said work will consist of two fifths of the best lime ordinarily used in the said place, and three fifths of the best or local sand, well crushed and blended with the said lime . . .

8^0

All of the chimneys will be built of good brick, eight *pouces* long by four wide, cleanly laid, and fully bonded with a mortar of lime and fine sand. Their flues will be well plastered with the same mortar as neatly as possible . . .

10^0

The roof will be covered with good Boston boards bevelled (*dElardé*) from two to three *pouces*, one on another, secured to each rafter by two nails, and the shingles laid on top will project at least four *pouces* in overlapping.

This *devis*, incidentally, reveals the peculiarities of the building materials at Louisbourg: an extensive use of brick and boards bought from the New Englanders. In the St. Lawrence valley brick was scarcely used except for making bake ovens where arches and domes of a small radius required its use. The *devis* would be favoured by the clientele of the masonry contractors, for many of them were educated people with some knowledge of building methods, thanks to laymen's guides such as Louis Liger's *La Nouvelle Maison Rustique*. Liger counselled his readers to start with "un plan exact" and "un bon devis" and to strictly adhere to both to avoid ruining one's self.[6] Once composed, the *devis* would be incorporated into the building contract or be annexed to it.

The builders at Quebec developed an expertise in using different types of stone from the region. The local limestone tends to break up into leaves like shale or slate when exposed to the weather. It, however, would make serviceable walls if it were laid, with the grain horizontal, in a thick bed of mortar. Even when used in this fashion, Quebec stone was found wanting. "The stone of this town," lamented one contract, " . . . is unfit for good bonding with mortar."[7] Limestone from Beauport, Cap Rouge and Cap Saint-Claude, which the locals sometimes called sandstone (*pierre de grès*), was used for facing, window and door surrounds, and decorative carving. The specialized uses of the different varieties of stone is revealed in a 1697 contract for an extension to a two storey house: "The exterior facing on the courtyard side and on the street side will be of Beauport stone, and the interior facing will be of stone from Le Cap; moreover

Maillou will be permitted to use some of the stones of the former walls, after demolition, to support and strengthen the said [new] walls raised upon them [their foundations]."[8] For the Estèbe house built in 1751-2 and still standing on Saint-Pierre street in Quebec's Lower Town, no expense was spared: "The outside of the dwelling's shell must be built of good limestone (*pierre de gré*) and good mortar, the inside can be made of Beauport stone or another type, provided that it is sound; all the doors, window frames and other cut stone-work must be done in Pointe-aux-Trembles greystone."[9] The Beauport limestone that was so popular for dressed work must have been impregnated with sulphur, for when he was at Quebec Peter Kalm observed that "the corners of the houses are made of a grey small grained lime-stone, which has a strong smell, like the *stink-stone*, and the windows are generally enchased with it."[10]

The building stone used by the Quebec City contractors was extracted by local quarrymen who were paid by the cubic *toise* delivered to the town or to the shore of the St. Lawrence River, where large, flat-bottomed boats with sails (*chaloupes*) loaded it for transportation to the town. The contractors and quarry-owners supplied the men employed in extracting stone with crowbars, mining irons (*barres à mine*), hammers, pickaxes, points, wedges and a trowel-like instrument called a "langue de boeuf."[11] Gunpowder was used in excavating foundations at Quebec and was also employed to loosen the rock in the quarries. The best stone came from well below the ground surface and it was roughly squared for the builder. Rounded fieldstones, particularly those of granite, were regarded as inferior building material since lime mortar did not adhere to them. The stone that came from the excavation for the foundations or was quarried within the town was used as fill between the inner and outer faces of the walls. In 1710 and 1727 the quarrymen of Quebec were ordered not to open new pits within the town and to keep clear of the fortifications, which they threatened to undermine with their digging and blasting.[12]

Pressed by the weather to build a house in a few months, the Quebeckers learned the value of "prefabricated components" in speeding the erection of a building. The phrase was alien to them but the concept was familiar. Dressed stonework was prepared over the winter and it was ready for installation by the spring. To survive, Canadian stonemasons were "maçons et tailleurs de pierre," which meant that they laid masonry in the warm months and, if they could find an employer, they cut and dressed stone in winter. At the end of the regular building season a few masons were engaged by contractors to prepare finished stonework for the coming year. How the less fortunate workers fared over the winter is not known. The mason who had been retained was given samples (*panneaux et échantillons*) as a model and, sometimes, a drawing of a desired mould-ing in profile. Payment for cut stone was by the linear *pied* with allowance for the complexity of the work.[13] The complete cycle of the mason's year is contained in an agreement between François De Lajoue and four Quebec stonemasons in 1695. They were to work for him "at dressing stone throughout the next winter . . . as well as laying stonework in the follow-ing spring, summer and autumn as long as the weather will allow it." Their employer would provide a covered working place that winter, and he left it to the workers to provide their own tools as well as the firewood needed to keep themselves warm. Their pay schedule was "12 *sols* for each foot of cut stone with moulding (*en Capucine*); 20 *sols* for each *pied* of dressed stone intended for windows, doors and fireplaces; and 55 *sols* for each workday employed in laying masonry, half payable in goods and the other half in money."[14]

The same unskilled workers and countryfolk who furnished builders with wood offered their services as limeburners and as carriers of sand and pebbles, which seem to have been used as a wall filler in Montreal. The lime used for making mortar, roughcasting and plaster was produced by heating crushed limestone in a conical oven. With the moisture and car-bon dioxide driven off, the material became quicklime, which was slaked with water after being removed from the oven. The hydrated lime was measured by the hogshead (*barrique* or *pipe*) and it seems reasonable to believe that it was packed into casks for delivery to the work site. Lime left exposed to the air would absorb carbon dioxide and revert to limestone, which was useless to the mason. To assure a constant supply of fresh and active lime in bulk for the construction of fortifications or a church, a lime kiln was built on the spot and tended by a full-time *chauffournier*.[15] Few private homes required such a convenience and the lime used in their construction was commonly burnt elsewhere. For the first Château de Ramezay at Montreal, two brothers were hired by the builder to supply "all the stone and lime he needs for the building . . . which they will be obliged to transport and deliver to the site."[16]

Chaux et sable was the standard formula for mortar and roughcasting. The sand could be had for nothing; one paid for its transportation. Al-though there were sandpits in New France, people preferred river sand that had been washed clear of clay and impurities. Sand deposits close to the towns were soon exhausted, and at Quebec, sand-gathering on the Petite Rivière Saint-Charles beside the town was first restricted and then forbidden altogether in the eighteenth century.[17] It is likely that the river-banks were being undermined by this activity. In 1683 a supplier cov-enanted with two Quebec builders "to convey and deliver to this town for them by boat (*barque*) . . . the sand gathered from the Montmorency Falls bank (*bature*); to wit, in 15 trips during the month of May."[18] A prominent Montreal builder, Paul Tessier, called Lavigne, engaged a worker in 1740 to "transport all the sand needed" for a house in the town from Côte Saint-Lambert across the river. The contractor supplied the man with "sa pirogue ou Canot" for this purpose. One wonders how much sand one could carry in a dugout canoe or whether it was worth the risk. Tessier did allow that "*quand Il ventera* (a delightful expression for windy weather) so that he cannot cross the river from the other side, he will cart pebbles from wherever he can find them." And to make things simple, the worker was to be paid for the sand by the cart-load (*tomberée*) – delivered by canoe, of course.[19] Three *journaliers* that Lavigne employed in 1749 had a better time of it; they were "to transport and convey all of the river sand" gathered "at Côte Mouille-Pied (Damp-Foot Shore), Saint-Lambert or La Prairie de la Magdelaine" in a large boat called a *bateau du roi* that belonged to the builder. On this occasion the measure was, appropriately, a boat-load (*battelée*) with the requirement that the labourers fill it up to the last wale (*préceinte*) before returning to Montreal. However, should they deliver pebbles, they would be paid by the cart-load.[20] At Quebec there was more consistency and the standard measure for sand and rubble-stone was a *chaloupée*, because a shallop was the most commonly-used vessel. A builder at Quebec, Joseph Routier, owned his own *chaloupe*, and in 1748 he took on two seamen to ferry stone in it for a one-third interest.[21]

All of these comings and goings impeded the operation of the port of Quebec. Debris was unloaded on the river bank as houses were demolished and the sand and stone delivered by the boatmen accumulated on the shore. It was wise not to leave wood piled at the water's edge, for if thieves did not take it, the river might. A load of oak beams that had been delivered at low tide was washed away with the high tide.[22] When the client was not responsible for delivering the materials from the shore to the building lot, carters did the job. There were plenty of carters and draymen in eighteenth century Quebec and they were paid by the cart-load at a rate that took into account the nature of the goods carried and the distance travelled.[23] Master builders and masons complained to Intendant Claude-Thomas Dupuy about the irreparable injury done to their projects by carters who wandered off the job "to engage in revelry (*faire la débauche*) or to go and serve other employers."[24]

With the mind's eye, let us imagine a construction site in the Upper Town of Quebec as it would have appeared in the 1750s. The muddy lot, right on the street, would be littered with stone chips and fragments of wood. Some of the debris belonged to a *colombage* house that formerly stood on the building lot. Carters, who had whipped their nags up the hill from the *grave* below, delivered piles of stone and sand that partially obstructed the roadway. A number of day-labourers were busily mixing sand and lime in wooden troughs, using water drawn from one of several barrels. Passing children, including those of the attorney-general, could not resist the temptation to push over a barrel, much to the annoyance of the workers who used the water to slake their thirst as well as the lime.[25] At Montreal one labourer was hired as a factotum "to help . . . as well as to smooth out the lime, mix mortar and carry water, and to break up (*piaucher*) the sand . . . , to put together the troughs (*bassins*) for crushing and mixing the lime."[26] The day-labourers climbed up ladders to deliver hods full of mortar to the masons, they cleaned and washed the craftsmen's trowels, they sharpened the cutting tools, and they beat the lumps out of the plaster. It was a demeaning occupation that most *Canadiens* disdained.[27] Unskilled colonials preferred to drive carts, which permitted them an independence of sorts. In 1687, when the colonial officials wanted to ship "two women of bad character" back to France, the Crown proposed instead "that they be put to hard labour on the public works, such as drawing water, serving masons, sawing wood, or other laborious occupations."[28] One cannot blame *Canadiens* for turning their noses up at what was considered punishment for whores.

It was essential to keep the masons supplied with mortar and stone so that their work would not flag. They began at ground level with a thick foundation wall two-and-a-half *pieds* wide and, as the wall rose up, its breadth was gradually reduced by a tapering exterior and interior insets (*retraits*) below each floor. The shelves thus formed were not used, as one might expect, to support the floor joists. The joists were usually seated in wall sockets a few inches above the inset. The height of each storey between floors varied from 6½ to 8 *pieds*. By the time the wall reached the top of the second storey – for masonry houses tended to be taller than wooden dwellings – it measured just 20 to 22 *pouces* across. As the wall was built up it was enclosed by a web of scaffold poles, ladders and boards that provided a platform for the stonemasons. Extra support for this shaky framework was gained from putlogs sticking out of holes left in the wall. These holes would be plugged with mortar once the scaffolding had been removed, and they can still be seen on old stone buildings. The masons perched on the scaffolding laid each course of quarry stone on a bed of mortar which they spread and smoothed with a trowel. Each stone was held up by a mason before the next space, gauged with the eye and, if necessary, trimmed with a hammer or hatchet to make it fit in place. A plumb line was kept handy to make sure that the wall was rising straight and true. The craftsman might take up his mallet, point and chisel to smooth off certain stones, such as the quoins at the ends of the walls which were larger than the other stones.[29] Such fine work was rarely done on the scaffolding.

The exterior face of the wall was built with the greatest care; the core might only be a helter-skelter mix of small rocks and mortar. The masons would point the mortar between the stones on the facade if the contract called for "les joints tirés en dehors." Often the joints were plastered over so that only the most prominent portion of the stones showed. One could go a stage further and cover the entire wall surface with a coat of roughcasting that still disclosed the shape of the stones beneath it. This was called "renduire les pierres apparentes." The ultimate finish, and remember that private clients could not afford an entire facade of cut stone, would be a flush surface of roughcasting with only the raised door and window margins left bare. The people of that period were not in love, as moderns are, with the coarse texture of rubblestone; they would cover it up if they could afford to do so. Under no circumstances would they have incised the joints between stones in the manner of some current "restorations" in the Province of Quebec. With traditional, soft lime mortar, that procedure would have accelerated the destruction of the wall by water and frost.

It was recognized that a construction site was a dangerous place. In France the workers above a street had to warn passers-by of the threat of falling stone by suspending a lath cross from their scaffold.[30] Loose entablatures were feared and they were to be secured with iron clamps.[31] Youth and folly were beyond legislation and no law could have foreseen the fatal consequences of a playful 15 year-old worker throwing a brick fragment at a young laundress as she knelt over her basin by the river. Instead of splashing her, as he had intended, the fragment ricocheted off the basin and struck the girl forcefully in the forehead; she died from the blow.[32] The building trades were subject to their own peculiar afflictions, too. Lifting heavy weights brought on hernias and falls from the scaffolding resulted in broken bones. For Michel Bouvier, a Montreal mason, that fall resulted in death.[33] An injury during Eastern Canada's short building season was a disaster for the victim: he could not earn anything and he had to pay medical and living expenses out of his own pocket.

An account of all the dealings of a major contractor was provided by Martial Vallet, a Quebec mason who was a foreman (*commis*) for Jacques Deguise, called Flamand, in the 1750s. In 1753, Vallet wrote, he had made up

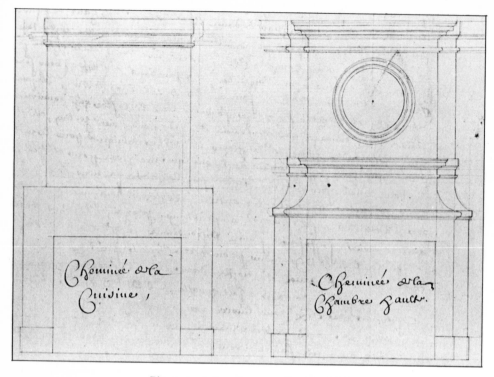

Plasterwork for a house at Quebec, 1679.

the accounts of his labourers and the amounts owed to them, which I paid. And each week I made several trips to the work sites to deliver accounts and chits (*les Ecrits*) to at least 40 men . . . . On the following Sunday I would draw up the accounts for his stonemasons, give a statement to each one and enter all of this in the account books – and this was done for more than 10 or 12 masons.

He did the same for Deguise's other employees: "his quarrymen, his carters, his boatmen (*chaloupiers*), and his stone suppliers, whether from Beauport, Ange Gardien, or Des Islets." Vallet also claimed to have delivered bills to clients and to have collected payments from debtors – all while doing a little masonrywork himself. He drew up an account of the work done at the Hôtel-Dieu: "comprising the height of the walls, the thickness of the roughcasting and plaster, the windows' dimensions and total footage of dressed stone" and so on. Vallet negotiated on behalf of Deguise with "his suppliers of hay and oats [for the draught animals], and with all those other persons with whom the said Flamand had dealings and for

EXPLICATION DE LA PLANCHE XXII.

I. Figure.
A Sonnettes.
1 Sole.
2 Fourchette.
3 Montans.
4 Mouton.
5 Bras ou Liens.
6 Rancher.
7 Jambette.
8 Poulies.
9 Cordages.

II. Figure.
B Singe.

III. Figure.
C Vindas.

IV. Figure.
D Verins.

V. Figure.
E Chable.

VI. Figure.
F Trousses.

VII. Figure.
G Rouleaux sans fin,
ou Tours Tarrieres.

VIII. Figure.
H Rouleaux.

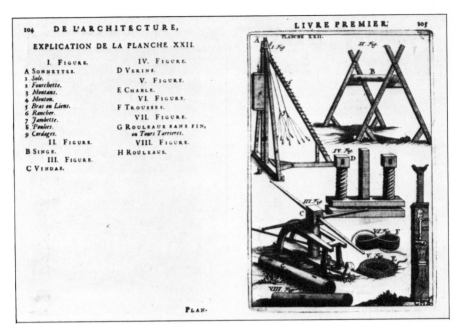

Plan-

The stonemason's tools.

EXPLICATION DE LA PLANCHE XX.

I. Figure.
A Chevre.
1 Bras de la Chevre.
2 Bicoq.
3 Clef & Clavette.
4 Entretoises.
5 Treuil ou Tour.
6 Leviers servant de Moulinet.
7 Moufle.
8 Chable.

II. Figure.
B Engin.
1 Plan de l'Engin.
2 Sole.
3 Fourchette.
4 Pernçon.
5 Jambette.
6 Moises.
7 Treuil ou Tour.
8 Bras du Treuil.

9 Rancher ou Escbelier.
10 Ranches ou Chevilles.
11 Selette.
12 Liens.
13 Fauconneau ou Estourneau.
14 Poulies.
15 Chable.
16 Piece de bois preste à monter
avec ce qu'on appelle
17 Halement.
18 Verboquet.

III. Figure.
C Escoperge, de la maniere qu'elle se met au dessus des Engins.

IV. Figure.
D Autre Escoperge qui n'est qu'une piece de bois, qu'on adjouste au haut des Gruaux.

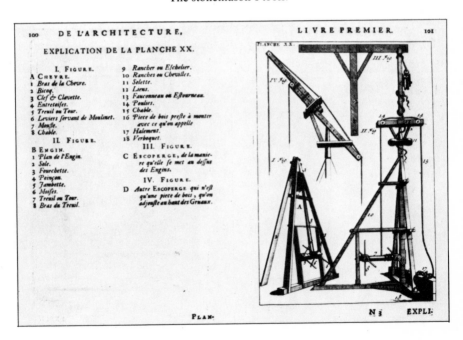

Plan-   N 3   EXPLI-

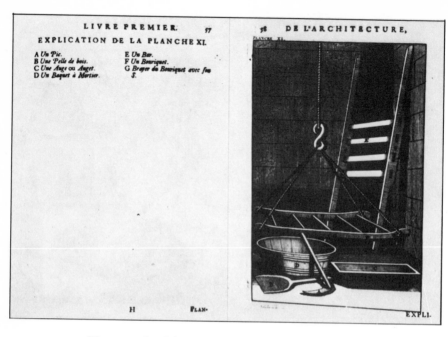

The mason's mixing, carrying and cutting implements.

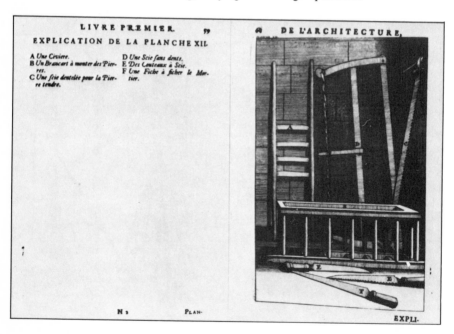

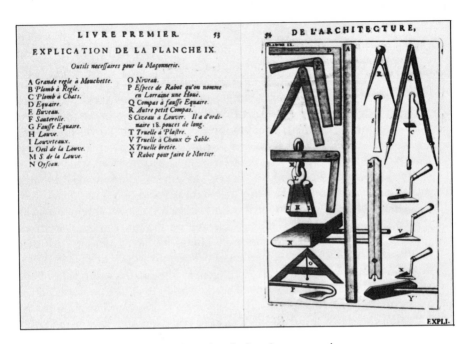

Hoisting and moving devices for construction.

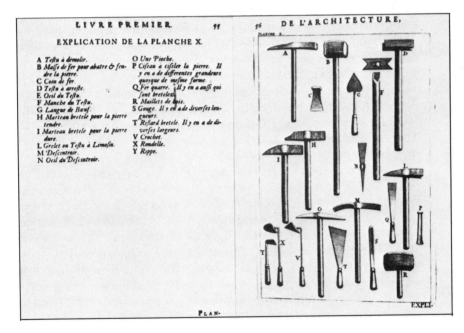

matters such as the contracts for and the distribution of bread, wheat, tobacco, hay [for bedding?] and meat for all of his employees." These duties were regularly performed for a number of years.[34] Vallet's statement revealed the scale of operations attained by contractors in the eighteenth century. Beyond some 50 construction workers at Quebec, Deguise retained the services of quarry-workers, boatmen and carters throughout the region. He bought forage from farmers for his horses and oxen and he purchased meat and bread for his men. Like many other employers at Quebec, he seems to have had a store from which he advanced goods on credit to his workers. These transactions made him more than a masonry builder; he was a merchant of goods and skills.

One of the enduring concerns of a contractor and his foreman was to keep the workmen out of the taverns and on the job. Carters, labourers, masons, carpenters and joiners were bound by their contracts "to work without a break until the completion of the said work" or face damages for any delay caused by their negligence. The law took the side of the employers and sought to keep the restless and bibulous *Canadiens* on the job. In 1676 tavernkeepers were forbidden "to give drink or food to any mason, carpenter, joiner or other worker under contract during the hours of work . . . without the permission of their clients or employers," nor were the workers permitted "to leave and abandon their tasks on days when work is possible without the permission of the home owner or general contractor."[35] For each infraction a fine of three *livres*, equal to the day's earnings of a mason, was payable by the contractor to the client. Masters were held to be legally responsible for the fines incurred by their journeymen, apprentices and indentured workers.[36]

A more punitive law covering all hired workers was incorporated into the 1727 building code, ostensibly in response "to the complaints . . . made by several contractors, master masons and other craft masters." The punishment for absenteeism and the consequent delays in the work fell directly on the guilty worker; masters were allowed to withhold a day's pay for any absence from work and to refuse payment for an incomplete piece of work. Workers hired by the month or year who wished to depart before the end of their term of service could be denied their wages. Moreover, at the time of contracting they could not demand more than one-eighth of their anticipated salary as an advance.[37] This ordinance applied equally to the workers of Montreal, who were not immune to these vices. 1685 was a peak year for the Montreal *bailliage* in dealing with wayward building craftsmen. In March a female innkeeper and a joiner were charged with encouraging the desertion of a carpenter employed by the Sulpician Fathers; in May another tavernkeeper was convicted of violating the regulations of the Quebec *Conseil souverain* against serving food and drink to masons and carpenters on workdays; and in June a mason was prosecuted for non-fulfilment of a contract because he had wasted his time in taverns.[38] Louisbourg had few alternative amusements to drinking liquor, and tavernkeepers there were repeatedly forbidden to serve drinks on workdays to craftsmen and soldiers employed in building the fortifications; nor were the innkeepers to accept goods from these men as payment for drinks.[39]

Let us assume that at our imaginary building site in eighteenth century Quebec we have an exceptionally sober group of craftsmen and that construction was proceeding on schedule. By June, the carpenters were seating the floor joists in the walls and the roof frame was being assembled in sections on the ground. Kalm marvelled at the simplicity of roofs in Quebec. "The private houses," he wrote, "have roofs of boards, which are laid parallel to the spars [i.e., rafters] and sometimes to the eaves, or sometimes obliquely . . . . The middle roof has two, or at most three spars covered with board only."[40] With the support of two stone fire gables, one could run a single ridge beam across without end framing; but what Kalm said was also applicable to country dwellings. There had been a simplification of roof frames in Canada and the second tie beam between rafters (*faux entrait*) was eventually discarded. Similarly, *Canadien* masons increasingly dispensed with a flatstone arch over openings and let the lintel carry the wall's weight. Colonial builders favoured simple and effective techniques.

We have not dealt with the roofer's trade in detail and with good reason. In Canada shingles were the mainstay of their occupation and when that material was effectively outlawed in the towns in the 1720s roofers lost much of their livelihood. Board roofing had been laid by carpenters and it continued to be done by them. The roofing contracts made before the proscription of wooden shingles in the towns of the St. Lawrence valley had a unique pattern. The roofer was given a sample shingle and those that he cut were to conform to the model, give or take four *pouces*.[41] We know very little about the standard size of wood shingles; a 1659 contract set their length at 16 to 17 *pouces*.[42] but that seems overly long since those used at Louisbourg averaged one *pied*.[43] The client could specify the size, since the roofer and his assistant split the shingles from wooden blocks themselves and tapered them with a draw-knife. The cedar that split so obligingly in one direction split damnably in the other: one roofer sought payment for the shingles made rather than for the area covered, explaining "that in using them many were broken."[44] Contracts usually stipulated that at least two nails be used to affix each shingle.

The Estèbe House in Quebec's Lower Town was one of the large-scale dwellings built in the 1750s by masonry contractors working in partnership.

Handwrought nails were expensive and they were used sparingly; when an old roof was being replaced the nails were salvaged. In 1683 a Quebec roofer contracted with a thrifty tailor "to roof his house with shingles . . . ; the said shingles will be laid in rows and be within four *pouces* of the sample given (*A quatre poulces d'Echantillon*); . . . the roofer, moreover, will remove the old roof boards . . . which he is to replace or [if still good] put back . . . using the nails that he recovered from the said old roof covering." For this service the roofer was to receive a sum of money, a new suit for himself and a grey cloth, hooded coat (*capot*) for his apprentice.[45] In Canadian roofing contracts a lump sum payment was preferred to payment by the square *toise* of roof surface covered; special prices were set for roofing dormers.

Intendant Dupuy's building code of 1727 was intended to force urban builders in New France to abandon shingles in favour of board roofs. Ten years before the Crown had given provisional approval to the use of roofing shingles at Louisbourg as a substitute for tree bark which was then outlawed.[46] On Isle Royale shingles were an improvement that was less destructive to local forests. Quite apart from legislation, the climate of Eastern Canada had forced a change in roof construction in the colony. The latticework used in France to support a roofing material, whether tiles or slate, was no protection against the cold winds and powdery snow of the Canadian winter. An impermeable, primary layer of close-fitting boards under the shingles or overlapping boards took its place. The 1727 code recognized this new technique in recommending "a first layer of tongue and groove boards, which will be covered by a second layer of boards running in the opposite direction and laid in such a way that they overlap one on another . . . . These boards will provide a snug roof for houses and will protect them from rain and blowing snow (*la poudrerie*) during winter."[47] The primary layer was also sealed by using bevelled boards, or even by caulking the joints. An additional seal against the weather was provided by plugging the space between the wall plate, on which the rafters rested, and the eave with *chaux et sable* plaster. A more unusual use of lime as a sealant and preservative appears in an agreement for a board and shingle roof near Montreal. With three *barriques* of quicklime, the roofer was to "entirely overspread and coat the roof with milk of lime and to whitewash the said roof and dormer with several layers of the said milk of lime and to apply it as thickly as possible."[48]

It is safe to assume that most shingles were made of cedarwood or, as at Louisbourg, of pine; it is less certain what the roofing boards were made of. In board roofing contracts and joinery agreements, it was ordinarily the client who supplied the wood and, therefore, it was not thought necessary to specify the type in the contract. Laying boards on a ridge roof was easily accomplished by July and it was now the turn of the joiner to add his touch to the house. The first thing he ought to have done after putting down the floor boards was to bring all of the lumber supplied by the contractor inside the building. Partially-demolished buildings and construction sites, when left unattended, were visited by scavengers who helped themselves to whatever materials and fixtures they fancied.[49] Crown projects suffered dearly from the theft of materials, wheelbarrows and tools[50] for, as a priest at Montreal explained, "most penitents believe that stealing from the King is only a petty offence."[51] Some of the pilferage was likely "an inside job" since building tradesmen felt that they were entitled to take home a few "scraps" of wood.

Woodshavings were the trademark of joiners. Carpenters rarely used planes; their work bore the marks of axe, chisel and adze. One of the initial tasks of the joiner was to use his planes to give a more finished appearance to the ceiling beams of the ground floor. If they were not cased, the beams were planed smooth and given moulded or chamfered edges. The upper surface of floors and the visible sides of panelling and partitions were likewise evenly planed or *blanchies*. They were not, it appears, painted or stained. All of this planing produced piles of highly inflammable shavings and in 1710 the joiners and coopers of Quebec had to be ordered to clean up the accumulated shavings after each day's work.[52] The joiners of New France, for their part, did not see anything wrong in working amid the litter of their trade with a lit pipe.

There were no full-time cabinetmakers in the colony and the furniture that was locally produced came from the hands of the joiners. Turning and wood sculpture were treated as natural offshoots of joinery. In 1745 a joiner at Pointe-aux-Trembles (Montreal Island) agreed to provide a weaver of the village with a full range of joinerywork and furniture, to wit:[53]

70 *pieds* of partitioning with concealed door casings, a straight staircase (*une Escallier plate*) for going up into the attic, an upper and a lower floor . . . with a straight staircase for going down into the cellar, four glazed mortise and tenon doors, one panelled mortise and tenon door in two leaves (*une d'assemblage en panaux a deux vollet*), an outside door, five solid doors with dovetailed casing, six casement windows with their shutters downstairs . . . , one attic window in the gable of the said house. The joiner is to plane the underside of three ceiling joists and their bearers (*palatrage*) as well as the window sills, [he will also provide] two wall cupboards, fully jointed and on either side of the fireplace, two

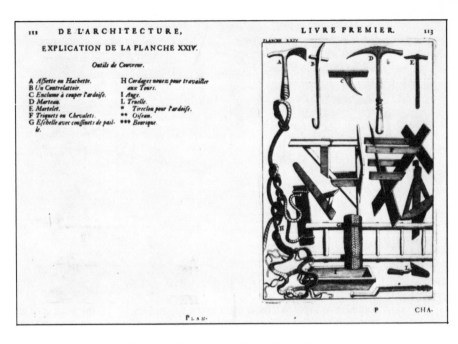

The roofer's tools and domestic hardware.

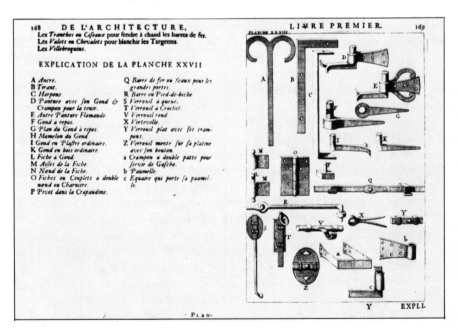

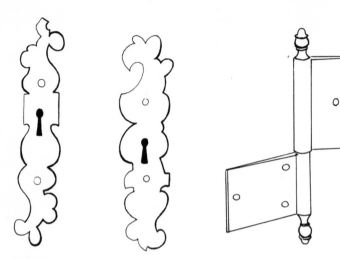

Key escutcheons for cupboards.

A *fiche à vase* was suitable for the main door or domestic cupboards.

cornices above the hearths, a table with turned legs . . . , the frame of an armchair with turned legs but without upholstery, and a sideboard built into the wall.

In the 1700s the planks of the upper floors were ordinarily tongue and groove or splined which, considering Kalm's remarks about the dirtiness of Canadian floors, would have been a good thing. Dirt and dust would easily sift through the cracks between butted (*à jointes carrées*) boards to the great discomfort of those below.

The finishing touch to our Quebec house came from the locksmith or metalworker. He made it possible for the contractor to deliver the new home "les clefs à la main." The small number of notarized contracts for domestic hardware is, perhaps, indicative of the tradition of salvaging the ironwork of old houses or the importation of metal work. For the security of the client, locksmiths were forbidden to duplicate keys without the lock owner's authorization.[54] There was in the ironwork of Canadian homes, as in all things in the house, a progressive refinement and an increase in the number of fixtures that a client could afford. In 1660 a wealthy Montreal trader, Jean Aubuchon, made do with "a complete lock suitable for locking a door . . . with a latch, a draw-bolt, and strap hinges and pintles . . . , as well as the ironwork for another door for the cellar, . . . the hardware for three windows consisting of strap hinges, hooks and eyes."[55] The hardware ordered by Joseph Istre represented an intermediate stage in the elaboration of fixtures. For the period of our imaginary house at

106

Quebec, we have the specifications draughted in 1751 for the home of François Daine, *lieutenant-général* of the Quebec *Prévôté* and comptroller of the *Compagnie des Indes*. A few extracts from the *devis* will illustrate the sophistication achieved in New France at mid-century:[56]

Firstly, the fittings on each door will comprise three vase-end hinges, a knob (*une pomme*), a rosette, and an iron latch; – all polished and fixed in place . . .

The hardware of each casement window will consist of three pairs of hinges and pintles, a two *pieds* long sliding bolt with guides, another bolt measuring eight *pouces* for the bottom of the window, four strap hinges and four pintles for the shutters, two S-shaped holdbacks [to hold them open], and an iron hook with eyes for [closing] the shutters; – all burnished and set in place . . . The fittings of the outside [i.e. main] door will comprise four strap and butt hinges (*pentures a Charnieres*), two retaining screws with nuts, a large ring knocker with its rosette, and an iron latch . . .

In the same manner that carved and panelled woodwork and cut stone proclaimed the owner's fortune and pretensions, the wrought iron that adorned the front door and windows advertised his status to all who passed by. M. Daine lived in an era in which there were contractors and craftsmen who could produce an *hôtel* expressive of his wealth and dignity.

NOTES

1. A.Q., G.N.R.F., F. Genaple, 20 août 1699.
2. François Blondel (ed.), *L'Architecture Françoise des Bastimens Particuliers* (Paris, 1685), avant propos, ii.
3. F. Blondel (ed.), *L'Architecture Françoise*, 347.
4. A.Q., G.N.R.F., F. Genaple, 29 août au 9 sept. 1703.
5. A.N., A.C., série G2, CLXXXIV (Conseil supérieur de Louisbourg), ff. 392-4.
6. Louis Liger, *La Nouvelle Maison Rustique*, 27.
7. A.Q., G.N.R.F., F. Genaple, 14 jan. 1700.
8. A.Q., G.N.R.F., L. Chambalon, 5 déc. 1697.
9. A.Q., G.N.R.F., G. Boucault de Godefus, 16 jan. 1751.
10. Peter Kalm, III, 104.
11. A.Q., G.N.R.F., J.E. Dubreuil, 4 avril 1730; N.F. 20, 26 avril 1751. The tools, as listed in the 1751 agreement, were "Une Crosse, Masses, deux pinses, quatre barre a mine, Un pique, et Une Langue de boeuf, et une Aerette, deux Coin, Et . . . la poudre necessaire."
12. E.O.R., II, 279, 318; I.O.I., I, 115-6.

13. A.Q.M., G.N.R.F., N.A. Guillet de Chaumont, 8 sept. 1732, 9 sept. 1732; A.Q., G.N.R.F., C. Barolet, 27 oct. 1734; L. Chambalon, 17 fév. 1702; J.E. Dubreuil, 27 déc. 1716.

14. A.Q., G.N.R.F., F. Genaple, 8 nov. 1695.

15. A.Q.M., G.N.R.F., J.B. Adhémar, 14 déc. 1734, 13 mars 1735, 3 mai 1735 (2); C. Maugue, 28 avril 1686; P. Raimbault, 7 juillet 1726; A.Q., G.N.R.F., C. Barolet, 3 oct. 1734; L. Chambalon, 2 mars 1704; J.E. Dubreuil, 21 avril 1722.

16. A.Q.M., G.N.R.F., A. Adhémar, 28 sept. 1704.

17. A.N., A.C., série Moreau de Saint-Méry, IX, f. 66; I.O.I., II, 118-9.

18. A.Q., G.N.R.F., P. Duquet, 12 avril 1683.

19. A.Q.M., G.N.R.F., F. Simonnet, 26 sept. 1740. The *canot* in question could have been the one ordered in March 1740 from Michel Lagu, a carpenter from Chambly. It was a monster 40 *pieds* long and 4 *pieds* wide and not a vessel that would be easily handled by one man. See A.Q.M., G.N.R.F., J.B. Adhémer, 6 mars 1740.

20. A.Q.M., G.N.R.F., F. Simonnet, 17 mars 1749.

21. A.Q., G.N.R.F., C. Barolet, 26 mars 1748.

22. P.A.C., M.G. 8, B 1 (Prévôté de Québec), III (1689), 379-380.

23. A.Q., N.F. 2, XXXVI, ff. 70-76 (Regulations for Quebec's carters, 21 April 1749).

24. E.O.R., II, 319.

25. P.A.C., C11A transcript, XXV, 32 (de Louvigny to the Minister, 21 Oct. 1706).

26. A.Q.M., G.N.R.F., B. Basset, 11 fév. 1665.

27. P.A.C., C11A transcript, XCIII, 327 (Bigot to the Minister, 21 Oct. 1749).

28. Edmund Bailey O'Callaghan (ed.), *Documents Relative to the Colonial History of the State of New York*. 15 vols. (Albany, 1853-87), IX, 323.

29. All of these tools are listed in a 1711 court case at Montreal. See A.Q.M., Juridiction de Montréal, Registre des Audiences, VII (1709-1713), ff. 714-714vo.

30. Edmé de Freminville, 201-2; Duchesne, *Code de la Police* (Paris, 1761), 201.

31. Edmé de Freminville, 243-4.

32. A.Q., N.F. 2, IX, ff. 105-106vo (25 août 1723).

33. Roland-J. Auger, *La Grande Recrue de 1653* (Montreal, 1955), 51.

34. A.Q., N.F. 20, No. 2076 (22 sept. 1757).

35. O.C.G.I., I, 194-5.

36. I.O.I., II, 111, 280.

37. E.O.R., II, 319-320.

38. A.Q., N.F. 21 (Juridiction de Montréal), III, ff.3-3vo. 10vo-11vo, 24vo-25vo.

39. A.N., A.C., série B, XLIV, ff. 552-552vo (8 avril 1721); série C11B, VI, ff. 29 (9 mai 1722); X, ff. 57 (25 avril 1728); XIII, ff. 3-4 (4 juillet 1741); série G2, CXCIII, registre 2, ff. 72vo-73 (24 avril 1755).

40. Peter Kalm, III, 104.

41. A.Q.M., G.N.R.F., B. Basset, 15 déc. 1659; M. Moreau, 25 fév. 1686; A.Q., G.N.R.F., L. Chambalon, 23 sept. 1692, 19 oct. 1695, 22 jan. 1696, 29 jan. 1696, 29 sept. 1701, 3 mars 1704, 18 déc. 1706, 11 juin 1707; P. Duquet, 2 mars 1682; F. Genaple, 29 avril 1683, 30 jan. 1696.

42. A.Q.M., G.N.R.F., B. Basset, 15 déc. 1659.

43. Linda Hoad, *Couverture en Bardeaux* (Fortress of Louisbourg manuscript report, 1968), 5. The shingles found on the site were "approximately 1.40' [English feet divided metrically] x .50' x .03' (butt) and .01' (feather) where taper present." See Richard E. Cox, "Wooden Shingles from the Fortress of Louisbourg," in *Bulletin of the Association for Preservation Technology*, Vol. II, Nos 1-2 (1970), 65-69.
44. P.A.C., M.G. 8, B 1, III (1689), 248-9.
45. A.Q., G.N.R.F., F. Genaple, 28 avril 1683.
46. A.N., A.C., série B, XL, ff.553vo-554vo.
47. E.O.R., II, 316-7. The same type of roof was used at Louisbourg "Pourque la neige ne puisse pas y passer dans les temps des grandes poudreries." See Linda Hoad, "Wood Shingles in 18th Century, Louisbourg," in *Bulletin of The Association for Preservation Technology*, Vol. II, Nos. 1-2 (1970), 62-65.
48. A.Q.M., G.N.R.F., F. Simonnet, 7 mai 1745.
49. A.Q., N.F. 21, XV, ff. 95-6 (Ordinance of 20 Sept. 1681 against thefts from the site of a church); R.A.P.Q., 1971, 136, 138, 140, 235, 307.
50. A.N., A.C., série B, XLIV, ff. 559vo-560 (Ordinance of 24 June 1721 against thefts from Crown projects at Louisbourg); I.O.I., III, 128.
51. Louis-Antoine de Bougainville (E.P., Hamilton ed. & trans.), *Adventure in the Wilderness* (Norman, 1964), 203.
52. P.A.C., M.G. 8, B 1, XII, 79 (Registration of a decree of March 1710 of the *Conseil supérieur*).
53. A.Q.M., G.N.R.F., F. Comparet, 22 fév. 1745. The French-Canadians have traditionally preferred casement windows to the sliding sash used by English-speaking settlers.
54. Edmé de Freminville, 540-2.
55. A.Q.M., G.N.R.F., B. Basset, 20 mars 1660.
56. A.Q., G.N.R.F., P. Lanoullier des Granges, 23 jan. 1751.

6

"If It Falls Down, It Will Have To Be Mended"

One of the standard clauses of a building contract was the contractor's vow to deliver the work "the whole sound, well and honestly made and finished, and subject to the inspection and approval of experts and knowledgeable persons upon whom the parties will agree."[1] The client promised, for his part, to make the payments to the builder as enumerated in the agreement. The final inspection before acceptance of the work would have been done as a matter of course for masonrywork done *à la toise*. Title IX of the *Coûtume de Paris* established the rules for the report of the customary two expert evaluators and a *toisé* or measurement of the work done. Private *toisés* have rarely survived and the majority of those that still exist were reports ordered by the courts to resolve a legal dispute. One of these fits the period of the hypothetical house at Quebec mentioned in the previous chapter. The report was submitted by Dominique Janson, called La Palme, and it reads:[2]

> I, King's Architect, certify that, having measured (*toisé*) both gable walls of the house, . . . the said gables are as follows: the southerly gable contains 9 *toises*, 5 *pieds*, 6 *pouces* [of masonry] and the northerly one has 12 *toises*, 4 *pieds*, 6 *pouces*, making a total of 22¾ [cubic] *toises*. – In witness of which, I have drawn up this report at Quebec on August 28, 1755.

In one case the mason was not permitted to cover up the masonry wall with roughcasting until the inspection had been completed.[3]

What recourse had a client if the house that had been inspected, accepted and fully paid for proved to be defective at a later date? In France the limits of a builder's liability were in dispute. In the eighteenth century Louis Liger asserted that "our maxim is that masons, carpenters, roofers and other such workers are answerable for their work for ten years after the date of completion, when the work is made of a solid material." The warranty of joiners, he wrote, was limited to six years.[4] The noted jurist Claude de Ferrière was of the opinion that a contractor could be prosecuted for gross defects within 20 years of completion of the building.[5] In Canada the extent of a builder's liability was even more uncertain and, in practice, his responsibility for workmanship was confined to the first few years after execution of the agreement. Explicit guarantees for a very short period were included in the odd contract. A Quebec roofer ensured his work for a year "lest the rain do any damage or pass through it."[6] A builder-contractor at Louisbourg only improved on this guarantee by adding one day.[7] These men were not giving anything extra to the customer; they were taking advantage of the uncertainty of the law to reduce their obligations to the period stated in the contract. It appears that, in the absence of an expressed warranty, a fault would have to be apparent soon after construction and it would have to be a major defect to be actionable in a court of law. In the case of a building that collapsed within one year of construction, there was no question that the builder was accountable.[8] In New France the obligations of the craftsman after that period were uncertain. In 1668 when a client at Quebec sought a court order against a stonemason to "rebuild a chimney that is about to collapse and may crush someone when it falls down, and because it was badly made," the artisan replied that, as the chimney had been built five years before, he was not responsible for it now.[9]

By reading just the notarized building contracts, one can be misled into thinking that house construction in New France invariably followed a smooth path. The court records are a corrective to this delusion. In Montreal, Trois-Rivières, Quebec and Louisbourg the conflicts of builder and client followed a similar pattern. The most frequently-encountered case is the claim of the building craftsman for the balance of what was owed him for work done. Next in frequency were the requests of customers to have an artisan compelled to begin or to complete the work that he had contracted to do. In 1689 the *Conseil souverain* made construction workers subject to arrest as well as seizure of property for non-fulfilment of a contract. It was claimed in the preamble of the law that "some contractors, stonemasons, carpenters, joiners and other craftsmen or day labourers undertake and bind themselves by contract to build and, after they receive the clients'(*bourgeois*) money, they do not fulfill their obligations. And they do this freely since most of them have no property and believe that no one can do anything against them."[10] This is a prejudiced explanation of a real problem for, on a close enquiry into the careers of individual builders, it appears that a few always undertook more projects than they could execute in a building season and that this was the cause for their delays and absences. This situation still occurs in the present. The source of the problem was more often complaisance, fear of losing a client or unjustified optimism than deliberate fraud. Less common than the two types of legal conflict cited above were the claims of builders against their suppliers of materials for delivery of wood, stone and quicklime; demands of the contractor's employees for wages and food; disagreements of builder and client over the form and method of payment and differences over the quality of workmanship.

A classic court case that combined many of these elements was heard by the royal court at Montreal in the winter of 1709-1710. At issue was a contract made in May, 1709, in which Jean-Baptiste Le Beau, a joiner, promised Edmé Moreau, a shoemaker, "two tongue and groove floors upstairs and downstairs, the upper one planed on one side alone and lower one left unplaned; the vestibule is to be planed smooth on both sides; the street door is to be held together by nailed cross-bars (*des barres a Cloux*) and the partition doors by dovetailed cross-bars; three partition walls will be planed on just one side; . . . [the joiner will also provide] four windows and four window frames to match the openings [in the walls.]" Le Beau's reward would be 75 *livres*, half payable in June and the balance due on August 15.[11] The second instalment was never fully paid and in December, 1709, the joiner initiated an action for the 30 *livres* still due him. The shoemaker's wife appeared as the defendant on her husband's behalf and stated in court that the work was subject to inspection, though this was not in the terms of the contract, and that the house still lacked the third partition wall. She also made the unwarranted complaint that the other partitions were not planed on *both* sides. The joiner let this misrepresentation of the agreement pass and then countered with his own grievance: the clients, he said, had failed to live up to their obligation to supply him with the wood he needed and had thereby wasted his time. After hearing both sides, the magistrate ordered the defendants to pay the 30 *livres* upon completion of the partition and its door, for which they would supply the lumber.[12]

When he heard of the judgement, Moreau the shoemaker would not let the matter rest. In January, 1710, he appeared before the court as a plaintiff against Le Beau. Moreau picked up his wife's point about the work being subject to approval and he requested a court order to have the joiner make good "the said work that is defective and useless" and to replace, at his own expense, "their wood that he wasted and had cut up in error." He said that he and his wife would pay the 30 *livres*, as ordered, but they demanded the right to deduct damages from the payment. The magistrate procrastinated; he repeated the previous sentence and put off consideration of the shoemaker's petition until a later, unstated date.[13] The court records do not provide the sequel to this story. The parties may have resorted to the system of arbitration provided by articles 184 and 185 of the *Coûtume de Paris*. The procedure was commonly used when the work executed had, in the opinion of one of the parties, departed from the contract. It might be an addition to the structure that necessitated an increase in the payment. An adjudication of the work would be made by two experts, one chosen by each party. If the matter were already the subject of litigation, the experts would take their oath of office before a judge, inspect the property and draw up their report on the spot, sign it and deliver it to the court within 24 hours of the inspection.[14] The Quebec *Prévôté* rejected one report because they had accepted food and drink from one of the litigants.[15] When the experts disagreed, the court could appoint a third to cast the deciding vote and then order a second inspection. If the legal dispute involved a *bourgeois* or gentleman against a craftsman and one of the assessors was already an artisan, the court was obliged to name a *bourgeois* as the third expert.[16] This was done, wrote one jurist, to offset the natural prejudice of craftsmen for one of their own kind.[17] The magistracy of France and her colonies seemed to have had no doubts about the impartiality of the gentry.

The Le Beau-Moreau case was quite typical of the housebuilding disputes heard in the courts of New France; its distinction is that it brings together so many of the familiar themes that appear separately in other cases. Here we have the artisan seeking payment for his work, the client's protest about incomplete and unsatisfactory work, and the complaint that the building materials were not provided when they were needed. The sequence of claim and counter-claim and the illogical reasoning of the disputants were repeated elsewhere a thousand times. In contrast to the adage that "a bad workman blames his tools," it might be said that craftsmen in New France tended to blame their materials for their non-fulfilment of a contract. When asked why he did not produce "a tongue and groove board roof" as desired, a joiner at Trois-Rivières replied in court that "the roof frame of the client's house was made for a horizontal covering and not board and batten (*de travers et non de bout*), and I was given roofing nails rather than long ones for boards." On these grounds he felt justified in having installed a lapped board roof (*couverture chevauchée*), that the client described as being of poor quality and susceptible to damage. With the experts' appraisal, the local court ordered the joiner to re-do the roof and, when he resisted, it authorized seizure of his property to cover the cost of having another craftsman do the work.[18]

In view of the disagreements that arose over work done under a nota-rized and written contract, it is marvelous that some people were so inno-cent as to undertake construction with only a verbal agreement. Since accords "de bon foi" were never registered, our knowledge of them de-pends on a few chance references. Though we only hear about those agree-ments that were violated, there may have been many informal accords that were fulfilled to the satisfaction of all concerned. Verbal agreements were more likely when the transaction involved less than 50 *livres* value and in poor regions such as the *gouvernement* of Trois-Rivières where registration might be seen as a luxury. If either party to a verbal contract failed to live up to his part of the agreement, the victim had a small chance of recovering something in the courts unless witnesses or the other party testified to the truth of the plaintiff's claim. Without written evidence, first-hand testimony by a reliable witness, or the defendant's admission under oath, the plaintiff's case was hopeless. In 1720 a contractor, Pierre Janson, called La Palme, appeared before the Montreal court with a re-quest to have a verbal contract to build a stone house upheld. He had received an advance payment from the client and, on the strength of this, La Palme had gone ahead and had made sub- contracts with carters and suppliers and he was stockpiling building materials on the site when he learned that his client, François Poulin de Francheville, had signed a notarized accord with another contractor to build the same house. In court the defendant admitted that he had had a "pourparler" with La Palme, but that when he had found that the builder had undertaken other pro-jects, Francheville had covenanted with the other contractor for his new house. The advance payment of which La Palme spoke was, according to Francheville, for some stone windows. The court accepted this explana-tion, for he was a man of property and a gentleman, and it dismissed the appeal of La Palme "since the plaintiff was unable to give proof of his agreement in writing."[19]

In 1701, again at Montreal, a carpenter built a house "les clefs à la main" on the mere understanding that he would be paid "as they will decide together or by arbitration." After the client had moved into the completed house, he told the carpenter "that he could not pay him, but that he would give him the interest on the price they will agree to or based on an evaluation to be made by two other persons." The estimators ap-praised the value of the home at 700 *livres* and the carpenter protested that his expenses, not to speak of the losses caused by the delay in payment, amounted to more than 1,100 *livres*. The court, after hearing that the litigants would name the same persons as experts and that the assessors would not change their original appraisal, dismissed the case and sentenced the carpenter to pay the court costs.[20]

Possession of a written and notarized contract, as we have seen, did not put aside all doubts and banish discord. It is evident that some parties did not comprehend the full meaning of certain traditional phrases and that others, upon reflection, regretted their undertaking. Payment as the work progressed (*au fur et à mesure que les ouvrages avanceront*) was a commonplace provision and one that was open to widely-differing interpretations. If the client delayed his payments the builder ran the risk of being sued by his employees and his suppliers for what he owed them.[21] The self-interest of both parties would incline them to come to different conclusions about the value of the work done before completion. The Quebec *Prévôté* ordered an evaluation of the work done by a joiner-subcontractor after he complained that he was being underpaid "au fur et à mesure."[22] One inexperienced customer was outraged when he realized that he was obliged to pay for masonrywork "tant plein que vide" and he refused to accept the measurement of what had been done.[23] His ignorance of a well-established principle makes one wonder just how many of those persons who signed or approved building contracts really grasped the full import of their undertaking. In 1702 Jean Boucher, called Belleville, the masonry contractor, asked the *Conseil souverain* of Quebec to release him from a contract made by his current partner, Pierre Janson, called La Palme. Belleville had withdrawn from the project with the objection that his associate had underestimated the amount of stonework required when he set the price. Belleville claimed to have been deceived, saying that he had never "been involved in any contract (*entreprise*) and that he was only a common stonemason who knew not how to read, write or do calculations, and that he could not be held accountable for La Palme's errors." This was a remarkable assertion by a man who signed documents and who was to become one of the major contractors in the colony. As for the 80 *livres* he had accepted from the advance payment, Belleville described the amount as "some money . . . for other joint concerns." It was, however, certain that La Palme's estimate was one-third short of actual requirements and the council voided all legal acts against Belleville for his failure to discharge his duties as La Palme's partner.[24] This leniency for a negligent contractor was exceptional.

The building disputes that came before the courts of New France do not bear out Louis Liger's claim that most legal problems in housebuilding originated with the deceptiveness of workers. A five-page section of *La Nouvelle Maison Rustique* was devoted to the "deceptions of workers in the matter of buildings" because, to quote Liger, "one is almost always cheated in the selection or in the use made of materials, and this is done as much through the ignorance and idleness of workers as by their bad faith."[25] The gist of his warnings was that whenever a craftsman was making something that would be hidden from view or subsequently covered up, he would be inclined to substitute inferior, second-hand, or undersized material for good timber, stone, mortar or tiles. The difference in value between what was required and what was put in its place would then be pocketed by the deceitful worker. Michel de Frémin's *Memoires Critiques d'Architecture* (1702), provided an ample "guide to all the tricks of faithless workers." The reader would be inclined to believe that house construction in Paris belonged to thieves, lying and flattering charlatans, and all manner of cheats bent on the ruination of the client. It was charged that "guileful stonemasons . . . will not spare any ruse or device to go beyond their contracts, so that a formal appraisal, which is the salvation of all workers and their ultimate resource, will be required."[26] Liger added that craftsmen always welcomed payment based on appraisals because "they have a secret way among themselves for ensuring that the estimation is in their favour."[27] The court records of New France contain no evidence that workers deliberately departed from the specifications of the contract in order to force an outside evaluation and a revision in the terms of payment. There were many incompetent artisans in Canada, but the same records describe none as dishonest as those pictured by de Frémin. It is not a matter of their being too skillful to be caught; building materials except for ironwork were cheap here and the fact that workers in Canada were better paid than those in France may have made such scrimping unnecessary.

André Félibien, author of *Des Principes de l'Architecture* (1676) provided a more tolerant explanation for the layman's dissatisfaction with building tradesmen. In his practical investigation of the manual crafts, Félibien anticipated the work of Denis Diderot in the following century. His object was to provide the layman with the principles and vocabulary of construction "for it is known that workers do not always execute things as one imagined them, and that they [often] do the opposite of what one wishes; and that is because they speak a language that is not well understood, and if one does not explain one's wishes in this same language, they will only have an imperfect conception of their employers' intentions."[28] The worst that Félibien encountered in his visits to various craftsmen was secretiveness and a tendency to take refuge in an obscure vocabulary. The same might be said of many professions in our own society!

The mistrust for craftsmen expressed by de Frémin, Liger and even Blondel was communicated to their readers and it permeated the upper classes of the colony. Clients harassed the builder by criticizing his procedures, by complaining that too many men were employed on the job, and by protesting that his mortar was "too dry and thinly spread."[29] Completed work was scrutinized for confirmation of the suspicion that the builder was defrauding the client with shoddy materials and poor workmanship. The complaints that did receive a hearing from the magistrates were of major defects, such as masonry "threatening . . . to collapse,"[30] or "walls that are too weak and are not of a suitable thickness, in short: they have not followed the terms of their contracts at all,"[31] or that "the said masonry work is very badly done, defective, and of bad materials, especially the said chimney which is in danger of falling down."[32] The mason whose work was the subject of the last complaint was also charged with leaving his work unfinished. Ill health may have been his excuse for he died in the midst of the litigation. The Montreal court decided that his estate should pay damages and should bear the cost of rebuilding the chimney as well as for having another man complete his work.[33] In the same vein, the Quebec *Prévôté* decreed that the widow of a masonry contractor should be responsible for finishing her husband's last project.[34] This pursuit of the craftsman beyond the grave reveals an inordinate reverence for the written contract. During the Seven Years' War the courts were equally rigorous in enforcing contracts when contractors pleaded that their employees had been called away for military service.[35]

We must admire the *sang-froid* of one Montreal stonemason when confronted by an irate client with a taste for dramatic gestures. The patron and a companion stood atop a recently-built brick oven that had shown signs of weakness and the customer cried out to the onlookers, "Behold my ruined oven," and "There is no one in Hell more unhappy than I." To this demonstration, the builder replied, "Well, if it falls down, it will have to be mended."[36]

NOTES

1. This particular quotation comes from A.Q., G.N.R.F., C. Barolet, 27 nov. 1752; the usual phrase is more terse: "fait et parfait au dire d'experts et gens à ce connaissants" or "sujet à visite."
2. A.Q., G.N.R.F., C. Barolet, 3 août 1755 (appendix to a contract for repairs to a house in accordance with the intendant's orders.)
3. A.Q.M., J.M., Registre des Audiences, VII (1709-1713), ff. 699vo-700.
4. Louis Liger, I, 175.
5. Claude de Ferrière, *Corps et Compilation de tous les Commentateurs . . . sur la Coûtume de Paris*, 4 vols. (Paris, 1714), IV, 364-5.

6. A.Q., G.N.R.F., P. Duquet, 2 mars 1682.
7. A.N., A.C., série G3, carton 2046, No. 55 (13 sept. 1733).
8. I.O.I., II, 242.
9. P.A.C., M.G. 8, B 1, II (1668), 403-4.
10. J.D.C.S., III, 330.
11. A.Q.M., G.N.R.F., M. Le Pallieur, 21 mai 1709.
12. A.Q.M., J.M., Registre des Audiences, VII (1709-1713), ff. 503-503vo.
13. *Ibid.*, ff. 507vo.
14. Julien Brodeau, *Commentaire sur la Coutume de la Prevosté et Vicomté de Paris.* 2 vols. (Paris, 1658), II, 691; Pierre Bullet, *Architecture Pratique*, 475-7; Claude de Ferrière, *Nouveau Commentaire sur la Coutume de la Prévóté et Vicomté de Paris.* 2 vols. (Paris, 1770), I, 399-403; Pierre Le Maistre, *La Coutume . . . de Paris*, 219-220. An example of an arbitration report that was filed with a notary is A.Q., G.N.R.F., L. Chambalon, 12 mars 1697 (depôt le 15 mars 1697).
15. Joseph-François Perrault (ed.), *Extraits ou Précédents, tirés des registres de la Prevosté de Québec* [1726-1756] (Quebec, 1824), 32-3, 41.
16. Claude de Ferrière, *Nouveau Commentaire*, 400-1.
17. Philippe Bornier, *Conférences des Ordonnances de Louis XIV.* 2 vols. (Paris, 1737), I, 174.
18. A.Q., N.F. 23, XIII (Trois-Rivières), ff.120vo-121, 124, 126vo-127.
19. A.Q.M., J.M., Registre des Audiences, IX (1719-1722), ff. 139-139vo.
20. A.Q.M., J.M., Bailliage: 1698-1702, f. 621vo.
21. A.Q.M., J.M., Registre des Audiences, XI (1726-1729), ff.95vo, 152; XII (1730-1732), ff. 624, 885.
22. P.A.C., M.G. 8, B 1, III (1689), 264-5.
23. *Ibid.*, XX-3 (1729), 461-3.
24. J.D.C.S., IV, 672-3, 684-5.
25. Louis Liger, I, 63.
26. Michel de Frémin, *Mémoires Critiques d'Architecture* (Paris, 1702), 187.
27. Louis Liger, I, 75.
28. André Felibien, *Des Principes de l'Architecture, de la Sculpture, de la Peinture . . .* , third edition (Paris, 1697), preface.
29. A.S.Q., Paroisse de Québec, No. 53 (c. 1685, Supplique des marguilliers à l'intendant contre Claude Baillif).
30. A.Q.M., G.N.R.F., B. Basset, 29 nov. 1672.
31. A.Q.M., G.N.R.F., J.C. Raimbault, 20 fév. 1734.
32. A.Q.M., J.M., Feuillets séparés, 3 sept. 1711.
33. See 32.
34. I.J.D.C.S., VI, 5.
35. For example, see A.Q., N.F. 23, XIII (Trois-Rivières), ff.80vo-81, 119vo, 191vo.; N.F. 20, (Prévôté de Québec, Pièces detachées) 17 aout 1756.
36. A.Q.M., J.M., Registre des Audiences, XI (1726-1729), ff.3vo-4vo.

Conclusion

What comes out of a study of housebuilding in New France is not just a sense of how people lived and a knowledge of their values. The mutations in building methods and contractual procedures also corresponded to the cultural and economic evolution of French Canada. The *colombage*, or half-timbered house, of the mid-seventeenth century was transplanted from provincial France as indeed were the immigrants who settled in New France and Acadia. The *pièces-sur-pièces* dwelling that appeared in the St. Lawrence valley during the second half of the seventeenth century was representative of the first generation of native-born *Canadiens. Pièces-sur-pièces* construction, in which squared timbers took the place of plaster or rubble fill within the wooden framework, was an adaptation to the new environment, a land of long winters and of plentiful forests. The economies made in building these houses and the roughness of the result bespoke the hardship and poverty experienced by the colonists in the seventeenth century. Though it later grew in size and in the refinement of the interior and exterior finish, this structure remained the basic rural house of New France. It was natural that the undeniably *Canadien* house of the early nineteenth century with its low, bellcast roof was constructed *en pièces-sur-pièces* and in stone. This indigenous house type developed in the countryside and not in the major towns.

Within the towns of New France local culture was subordinated to external influences. Metropolitan fashions were followed in Quebec and Louisbourg and the concern of the authorities with fire prevention imposed a stylistic discipline on urban housing. The massive fire gables and the tall, broad chimneys could not be ascribed to the builder's fancy except when these forms appeared in the countryside in the eighteenth century. What was functional in the city had become fashionable among the rural

This nineteenth century *pièces-sur-pièces* farmhouse at Oka was distinctively Canadian in form and structure.

folk. The "Canadianization" of urban dwellings was, however, visible in structural changes: the front vestibule and the snug roof that were to keep out the cold air and the blowing snow. In Canada there was also a general simplification in roof frames and masonry technique.

The number and size of stone dwellings increased in proportion to the prosperity of the colonials and the stability of New France. The number of urban houses built of stone became notable in the 1680s. Masonry construction did not triumph in the towns, however, until the eighteenth century, first at Quebec and then in Montreal. It was an economic barometer and its reading for the period from 1720 until 1755 was wealth and security. The colony was no longer a precarious outpost in the New World; it was a well-established community whose members knew prosperity as well as poverty.

If one doubts the argument that the history of French Canada was written in its architecture, one need only look at Louisbourg, a city nearly as large as Quebec and equally prosperous. It had its own building technique, construction *en piquets*, and the dominant medium was wood, a mate-

Krieghoff's Jolifou Inn was based on those rural dwellings that used the urban fire gable as a decorative feature.

rial as temporary as the population, whose roots in North America were shallow. To build in stone was not only a privilege of the well-to-do, it was also a commitment to the new land. In the valley of the St. Lawrence the domestic house and the arrangements that accompanied its construction marked off the stages by which the *Canadien* went from being a French immigrant to a colonist, from being a colonist to a well-established, provincial type within the French empire, and finally emerging in the early nineteenth century as something unique, a part of *la nation canadienne*. More than a house was being built; a nation was also being built.

Appendix A

Glossary of French Terms

Accoyau – corbel.

Architecte – a builder capable of drawing and interpreting measured plans; often with a knowledge of the classical orders of decoration.

Ardoise – slate.

Arpent – measure of length equal to 191 feet, 9 $9/16$ inches or 54.8 metres; the square *arpent* was the standard unit for measuring land area, and it equalled $5/6$ of an acre or 0.205 of a hectare.

Au fur et à mesure – in proportion to the work done.

Aveu et denombrement – seigneur's acknowledgement of lands held from his lord.

Bailliage – lower court of the seigneurs of Montreal Island.

Bardeau – wood shingle.

Barre à queue d'aronde – dovetailed cross-piece or cleat on a door or shutter.

Barrique – a large measure of volume, a hogshead.

Blanchi – planed smooth.

Bousillage – mud walling.

Cave – cellar.

Chaloupe – large, open boat propelled by sails and oars.

Charpente – a building frame in wood; used for half-timbered structures at Louisbourg.

Chassis – frame, used primarily for wooden sash or cut stone surrounds for windows.

Chauffournier – a limeburner.

Chaux – burnt lime used for mortar and plaster.

Chevron – rafter.

Chevauché – overlapping, when applicable to boards.

Cloison – partition wall.

Colombage – half-timber construction in which the space between the wooden timbers in the walls is filled with another material.

Conseil souverain/supérieur – highest court at Quebec serving all of New France except for Ile-Royale and Ile Saint-Jean, which were subject to the *Conseil supérieur* at Louisbourg.

Contre-mur – additional wall to protect a shared wall or adjoining property from heat or pollution.

Contrevent – shutter.

Coûtume de Paris – the traditional civil laws of Paris, as codified in 1580, which were extended to the French colonies.

Coyau (Coyaux) – furrings on rafters giving the roof a bellcast eave.

Crépi – roughcast wall covering.

Croix de Saint-André – diagonal and intersecting braces between the trusses of a roof frame.

Devis des ouvrages – list of specifications for a building.

Embouveté – with tongue and groove.

Enduit – plaster wall covering.

Fiche – hook for a hinge; often a hinge itself.

Filière – purlin.

Frêne – ashwood.

Galerie – elevated wooden walk or balcony on the outside of a house.

Gobetage – rough plastering.

Gond – pintle for a hinge.

Grave – beach; two landing places at Quebec's Lower Town were known by this name.

Hôtel-Dieu – hospital.

Joints tirés en dehors – tuckpointed mortar between stones of a wall.

Journalier – day labourer employed in unskilled tasks.

Lait de chaux – whiting of lime, or whitewash, a byproduct when excess water is used to slake quicklime.

Lambourde – joist, usually for supporting a floor.

Languette – chimney flue divider, sometimes used for splines.

Livre – highest unit used for financial accounting in the French regime; also used for a pound weight.

Loquet à poignée – thumb latch for opening doors.

Lucarne – dormer.

Madrier – heavy plank.

Marché – contract.

Marché en bloc – building contract for a fixed, total price; also called *marché en tâche* (cf. *marché à la journée* - payment by the day).

Marché les clefs à la main – contract for a completed house.

Minot – a volume measure for grain equal to 1.05 bushels.

Mur mitoyen – shared or common wall between properties, including a wall common to two adjoining houses.

Noyer – walnut wood; *noyer tendre* is butternut wood.

Ordonnance – a regulatory decree, usually addressed to a particular situation, issued by royal authority.

Patte – iron pin to affix woodwork to masonry.

Penture – strap hinge.

Pièces-sur-pièces – a form of wooden construction in which the walls of a framed building are made of horizontal, squared timbers whose tennoned ends are slotted into grooves in the upright posts of the frame.

Pied – measure of length equal to 1 foot, 13/16ths of an inch or 32.48 centimetres.

Pierre de grès – sandstone; applied to limestone in the Quebec region.

Pierre piquée – stonework roughly finished with a mason's point.

Pierre taillée – stonework smoothly finished with a chisel.

Pierres d'attente – stones left projecting from a gable wall to support future lateral walls.

Pieux – stakes, posts planted in the ground.

Pignon – gable; applicable to the entire end wall as well as the gabled top.

Pipe – cask containing 1½ hogsheads or *muids*.

Piquets – round posts used in making walls in the French settlements on the Atlantic coasts of Canada.

Pistole – a gold coin of French, Portuguese or Spanish origin worth about 11 *livres* of account in the seventeenth century.

Planche – thin board.

Plancher – floor; *plancher haut* in a one storey building means a ceiling.

Plate bande – flat stone lintel over a hearth opening.

Pot de vin – a gratuity given by the client to the builder.

Poteau – post, used for the studs and corner post in a building frame.

Pouce – measure of length equal to 1 and 1/16 inches or 2.7 centimetres. Twelve *pouces* make one *pied*.

Poutre – heavy joist or beam.

Prévôté – royal lower court at Quebec and Louisbourg.

Prûche – hemlock tree; spruce on Ile-Royale.

A queue d'aronde – dovetailed joint.

Renduire à plain – smooth roughcasting over masonry; *renduire les pierres apparentes* is a complete covering that discloses the shape of the stones beneath it.

Retrait – inset or setback on a wall.

Saillie – projection on a building.

Soliveau – light joist or rafter.

Solle – sill beam.

Soupiraux – ventilation openings in a foundation.

Tambour – covered vestibule just inside or outside the main door.

Tant plein que vide – measurement of the volume of a wall that treats openings as part of the solid portion.

Targette – sliding bolt to secure the top or bottom of a window casement in the closed position; it is usually long and vertical.

Toise – a measurement of length equal to 6 feet, 4¾ inches or 1.95 metres. Six *pieds* make a *toise*. The cubic *toise* was used to measure masonrywork and the square *toise* was employed in measuring plasterwork, roughcasting and, occasionally, roofing.

Toisé – formal measurement and appraisal of masonry construction in order to establish its value. The term was also used for an evaluation of other forms of construction in materials other than stone.

Verrou – draw bolt across an opening panel to secure a window, shutter or door from the inside. It was usually horizontal and short in comparison with a *targette*.

Vin de marché – wine or liquor given by the client to a craftsman to seal an agreement; a euphemism for a gratuity given to the artisan.

Appendix B

Principal Contract for the Jean-Baptiste Forestier House*

Marché de La batisse de La maison de S[ieu]r. Jean Bt. forestier Le 20e. Xbre. 1728. Pardevant Le Notaire Royal en La Juridiction Royale de Montreal, Soussigné resident a Villemarie, furent presents Sieur Jean Baptiste forestier M[aîtr]e. Chirurgien Et Sieur Jacques Dielle Me. forgeron, demeurants tous deux en cette Ville, de present y estant, Lesquelles de Leur bon gré et volonté ont fait et accordé Les Conventions de bonne foy qui Suivent, Cest a Scavoir, que Le dit Sieur Dielle S'oblige faire fairre Et bastir une maison Sur un Emplacement De Quarante deux pieds de front Sur La rue Nôtre Dame Sur sa profondeur au Sieur J Bte. forestier a ce present et acceptant pour Luy Ses hoirs et ayans Cause; La ditte maison Sera bastie de Pierre de La Contenance de trente Sept pieds Seulement Sur La ditte rue Notre Dame, avec cinq pieds qui resteront Sans bastir dessus pour Un passage pour entrer dans La Cour, Et Sur La profondeur trente cinq pieds, Led[it]. Bastiment Sera d'un Etage qui Sera Le rets de Chaussée avec Les greniers au dessus, Le pas de sa porte Sur La rue Notre Dame Sera exaucé et Sorty hors terre de deux pieds et demie, Les planchers Seront de huit pieds et demie de haut d'un plancher a L'autre /page 2:/ Et au dessus des poutres La muraille Sera exaucé de trois pieds et demie, Il y aura deux soupiraux qui Seront taillez comme Ceux de toussaint La Marche, avec cinq ouvertures Sur La ditte rue Notre Dame qui Seront deux portes et trois fenestres ainsy places Selon Le plan qui en a esté dressé, Et Sur Le derriere de Ladite maison, Il y aura aussy une porte et quatre fenestre, en outre une autre fenestre dans Le pignon du Costé du Nordest, Et toutes Les dittes fenestres dudit Bastiment Seront de cinq pieds et demie de haut et trois pieds de Large La porte du millieu Sur La ditte rue Nôtre Dame Sera de trois pieds et demie de Large, et Les deux autres portes de trois pieds Juste aussy de Large et Seront de La hauteur du Nivau de La couverture des Croisées, Et La pierre de taille Sera a detachement [insertion: Sur Le Devant] et Le Coin du Nordest Sera piquez dans Lesquels [i.e. le coin] Il Sera passé deux gros gonds pour pendre La porte de La Cour, Il y aura aussy dans La ditte maison trois cheminées Separées dont deux a detachement, Et dans La Chemineé de La Cuisine Il y posera un bon Crampon

*Archives du Québec (Montréal), Greffes des notaires du régime français, Nicolas-Augustin Guillet de Chaumont, 20 decembre 1728.

de fer pour y pendre une potence Et dans Les deux autres Cheminées Il y Sera
fait deux feilleure et une retraitte au mur d'environ un pouce, Il y aura aussy Six
/page 3:/ Lambourdes Lesquelles Seront Cannelé pour recevoir un premier
plancher qui Sera de Cedre avec dans tous Les Joins un fillet de mortier [inser-
tion: de Chaux] et pardessus sur Le plus haut des pieux du dit premier plancher
un pouce de terre, Les Entraits Seront a Sept pieds du plancher et Les Aiguilles
auront au moins dix huit pieds, Quatre ferme et Les Jambes de force Seront
prise Si faire ce peut et Si cela Se rencontre dans La muraille et dans Le bout des
poutres, Il y aura au grenier cinq Lucarnes trois au premier Etage dud[it].
grenier et deux aux Entraits, Et Les arrieres Voutes de touttes Les ouvertures
Seront de pierre, dans La muraille au rets de Chaussée Il y aura aussy quatre
Armoires [insertion: Si La place S'y trouve pour Les Placer] qui Seront chacune
de Six pieds de haut et de quatre pieds de Large C'est a dire Le basty Seulement
des dittes armoires avec trois paires de fiches a chaque Croisée et un petit
verroux Sur Le millieu du battan, Les targettes des fenestres Seront de deux
pieds et demie de Long en haut Seulement, Les deux portes de dessus La ditte
rue Notre Dame Seront brisées a panneaux couverts avec trois fiches a chacune,
Les feuyez Seront piquet (sic) et Il mettera un Evier dans La Cuisine et Le
devant Sera de pierre a parment La planche de La Couverture chevauchera de
quatre pouces, Et en outre La menuiserie dans toute La ditte maison ou Il y aura
quatre quatre (sic) portes /page 4:/ dAssemblage et Les autres Seront Unies
dont une Emboëture en haut Et barre a queues en bas, Le Pignon du Costé du
Sorouest Sera fait mitoyen avec Mr. Istre qui est Voysin dudit Sr. forestier qui
sera basty sur Les fondements qui Sont desja faits de Lancienne maison, Et Le
Pignon du Costé du Nordest Sera augmenté de deux pieds de Longueur Sur
Lad[it]e. rue Notre Dame Et La Cave [crossed out: demeurera comme elle est],
Sera exaucé au nivau du plancher, Comme Il y a actuellement une vielle maison
basty Sur Le dit Emplacement ou Led. Sr. forestier veux et entend que Led. Sr.
Dielle Luy fasse bastir La ditte maison dont Ils Sont convenus par ces presentes
Led. Dielle S'oblige a La faire demolier (sic), [crossed out: Et] Sur Le devant
qui donne dans La ditte rue Notre Dame Jusques au Nivau des terres et par
derriere Jusquaux fondements Sans estre obligez a faire La ditte Cave, Pourra
Led. Dielle faire Servir Les vieux materiaux qui Seront bons et propre pour cette
Effet, Sans toutes fois mettre dans Les Chambres dud. Bastiment de vieux bois
pour Les Cloisons; Abandonnant pour cet Effet Led. Vieux Batiment dans Son
Entier tel qu'il est presentement et qu'il Se poursuit et comporte aud. Diel, En
outre Crespir par dedans La ditte Cave, Et Led. Sr. Diel a reconnû et Confessé
avoir fait Led. Marché promis et promet par ces presentes aud. Sr. forestier a Ce
present et acceptant de faire et parfaire La ditte maison bien et duement /page
5:/ au dire d'Experts et gens a Ce Connoissans, tous et chacuns Les ouvrages de
maconnerie, Charpenterie, Couverture, menuiserie, Serrurerie, plancher, Cloison et autres Chose qu'il convient faire pour Le bastiment et Construction
entierre et parfaitte de La ditte maison Scize rue ditte Notre Dame de La
Contenance de trente Sept pieds Sur La ditte rue Et trente cinq Sur La profondeur Suivant Le dessein et Le plan qui en a esté fait et qui a esté presentement Signé et Paraphé par Les dittes parties et Notaires soussignez Lequel Sera
remis es Mains dud. Notaire pour par Luy estre represente pour Visiter Les
ouvrages toutes fois et quantes qu'il plaira aud. Sr. forestier ou au porteur de Sa
procuration pour cet Effet en son absence, a Commencer a travailler aux dits

ouvrages des Le mois d'Avril prochain et continuer Incessamment a y travailler avec bon nombre douvriers Suffisans Sans discontinuation et rendre Le tout bon et Valable et Livrer Les Clefs a La main dud. Sr. forestier ou procureur pour Luy, a peine de tous depens dommages Et Interest. [insertion: Led. Sr. Diel n'est pas tenu de parachever La ditte maison L'année prochaine mil Sept cent vingt neuf mais Seulement en rendre La moitié Logeable pour y Loger ceux que Led. Sr. forestier Jugera apropos au Jour de La toussaint au plus tard de Lad'e. année] Ce Marché et promesse faits moyennant La Somme de deux mil cinq cents Livres pour tous Les dits ouvrages de Maconnerie Charpenterie &c. payables Scavoir Quatre paquets de Castor ou Pelleteries dans Le Cour de L'Etée de Lannée prochaine, Plus Cent minots de bled dans Le Cour de Cet hyver Et Le restant en marchandises au prix du Detail a fur et a mesure qu'il en aura besoin [insertion: Et qu'il travaillera aud. Bastiment], et en Cas que Le dit Sr. Dielle n'aye pas besoin de toutes Lesd'es. merchandises. Et qu'il Veuille attendre Jusques a Lannée mil Sept cent /page 6:/ trente Led. Sr. Dulonpré Le payera en Castor ou pelleteries [crossed out: au Choix dud. Diel], Led. Diel S'oblige aussy de faire bastir un four au lieu que Le Sr. Dulonpré Luy designera qui Sera de deux minots; Et en outre Les arrieres Voutes generallement Seront de pierre toutes, En outre fera Led. Dielle tous Les Contrevent, des fenestres, remplira Sous Le plancher a plein, fera Le Dressoir, Les tablettes du magasin Et Rasera La muraille Jusquau rets de terre, renduira La Cave en dedans, Et Lapuy des fenestres Sera un peu versé en dehors, Et Sur Laditte Somme de deux mil cinq cents Livres Led. forestier donnera aud. Dielle Cent Livres en Lettres de Change ou pelleteries Car ainsy Son Convenus Les dittes parties et pour L'Execution des presentes Led. Sieur forestier a Esleue Son domicille Scize rue Notre Dame et Led. Dielle Scize rue St. francois où ils Veulent et Entendent que tous actes exploits Et signiffications Leurs Soient fait; Promettant &c. obligeant &c. renoncant &c. fait et passé audit Villemarie en L'Etude du dit Notaire Lan mil Sept cent vingt huit Le Vingt Decembre apres midy presence des Sieurs Charle Quenneville Me. tailleur et Pierre Busson Subtil Aubergiste temoins demeurants au d. Villemarie qui ont avec Les dittes parties et Notaire Signéz apres Lecture faitte Suivant L'ordonnance Neuf mots barez Sont nuls

signed: Jaque dielle
                              JB:forestier
                              subtile
                              P. Quesneville
                              Chaumont n[otaire]. r[oyal].

/page 7:/

L'an mil Sept cent Vingt neuf Le treisieme Jour d'Aoust apres midy est comparû en L'Etude du Notaire Soussigné Le Sieur Jean Baptiste forestier acquereur au marché cy devant Lequel ayant Jugé apropos pour son Utilité de Changer quelque Chose a La Batisse de La maison dont Il est parlé dans le dit marché, dont LEntrepreneur Est Le Sr. Diel, ce present et acceptant, Sont convenus qu'en presence des tesmoins Soussignez, que Le premier [crossed out: Bail] Plan qui estoit resté en notre Etude annexé a La minutte du dit marché Sera Biffé et de nul Valeur et Pour cet Effet [crossed out: en] a esté fait un autre Plan Signé La Brosse et Signé desdittes parties pour estre par Ledit Diel Suivy de point en point [insertion: a L'exception d'une poutre qui a este rangé de Costé avec la

Cheminée d'environ d'un demie pieds], Laditte Augmentation Sera d'une Cheminée au milieu de Laditte maison avec Son fouier, fera aussy Les Cloisons et Serrures, portes, fondement, Elevation des pignons audessus de la Couverture qui est deux pieds d'Elevation, Et Les armoires qui Sont marquez Sur ledit Plan Sans que ledit Dielle Soit obligé de faire Les placars non plus que L'augmentation du pignon qui est mitoyen, Et pour laditte Augmentation Ledit sieur forestier S'oblige bailler et payer audit Sieur Diel La Somme de quatre Cents Livres en marchandises telle qu'il est Speciffié dans le marché cy devant a peine &c. Sous L'obligation et hypotecque de tous Ses biens meubles et Immeubles presens et avenir Et pour L'Execution des presentes Lesdittes parties ont Esleu Leur meme domicille comme au marché cy devant Car ainsy &c. Promettant &c. fait et passé audit Montreal Ledit Jour et an que dessus presence des Sieurs Dominque Genson Lapalme et Jacques Guy dit Chateauneuf tesmoins demeurants audit Montreal qui ont avec Lesdittes parties et Notaire Signez Lecture faitte suivant L'ord[onnan]ce. / deux mots barez sont nuls
[signed:]

JB. forestier
jaque dielle
J. Guy
Lapalme fils
Chaumont n.r.

/page 8:/

L'an mil Sept cent vingt Neuf Le treizieme Jour d'Aoust apres midy est comparû en L'Etude du Notaire soussigné Le Sr. Jacques Dielle Entrepreneur de la Batisse de La maison mentionné au marché de Lautre part Lequel a reconnû Et confessé avoir receu du Sieur Jean Bte. forestier La Somme de deux mil cinq cents dix livres onze Sols a Compte des deux mil neuf cents Livres que Ledit Sieur forestier Luy doit pour La Batisse de Sa maison de laquelle Somme de deux mil cinq cents dix Livres onze Sols Ledit Diel tient quitte et descharge Ledit Sieur forestier et tous autres [insertion: Comme de La moitié du pignon que Le Sieur Istre devoit payer audit Diel dont Il Le tient quitte aussy et Le descharge, L'autre moitié du pignon Led. Diel estant obligé de le faire Sur Le marché des dits deux mil neuf cents Livres] dont quittant &c. fait et passé aud. Villemarie Estude dudit Notaire Les Jour et an Susdit presence des Sieurs Charles quesneville et Pierre Busson Subtil tesmoins demeurants audit Villemarie qui ont avec Lesdit Srs. Dielle forestier Et Notaire Signé Lecture faitte Suivant Lord'ce. [signed:]
jaque dielle
Istre
P B subtille

JB:forestier
C. Quesneville
Chaumont n.r.

Pardevant Le Notaire Susdit et Soussigné fut present ledit Sieur Jacque Dielle Entrepreneur au Contrat de la Batisse de lautre part de present en cette ditte Ville de Montreal lequel a reconnû et Confessé avoir receu comptant dud. Sr. Jean Bte. forestier la Somme de [crossed out: deux mil] trois cents quatre Vingts neuf livres neuf Sols pour parfait payement de la batisse de la maison que led. Dielle a fait au d. Sr. Forestier Suivant et Conformement au devis et marché de l'autre part, de laquelle Somme de trois cents quatre Vingt neuf livres neuf Sols avec Celle de deux mil cinq cents dix livres onze Sols qui sont Les dittes deux Sommes entieres faisant celle de deux mil neuf cents livres prix de la batisse de Laditte maison. Led. Dielle tient quitte et descharge led. Sr. forestier et tous autres, de mesme Ledit Sr. forestier tient quitte et descharge led. Dielle de tout ce qui pouroit avenir Et Se percevoir en laditte Batisse, Et Se tiennent respectivement quitte lun envers lautre Car ainsy & c. Promettant chacun en droit Soy &c. renoncant &c. obligeant &c. fait et passé aud. Montreal Estude dud. notaire L'an mil Sept cent trente deux le huit Juin apres midy presence des Sieurs Jean Bte. Senet et Claude Collet tesmoins demeurant audit Montreal qui ont avec les dittes parties et Notaire Signé lecture faitte / deux mots barés nuls ./.

[signed:]
jaque dielle

JB: forestier   Collet
Jean Bte Senet   Chaumont nr.

[Paul Jourdain La Brosse's revised floor plan, measuring 32 by 41 cm., is annexed to the contract with its amending clause and appended two receipts.]

Bibliography

Building Contracts Consulted

SHARED GABLE AGREEMENTS:
Archives du Québec, Greffes des Notaires du Régime français [hereafter A.Q., G.N.R.F.],C. Barolet, 23 juin 1733; J.E. Dubreuil, 17 mai 1724, 27 avril 1728, 23 juin 1728; J. Pinguet, 16 mars 1728.
Archives du Québec (Montréal) [hereafter A.Q.M.], G.N.R.F., N.A. Guillet de Chaumont, 10 août 1729.

FOUNDATION EXCAVATORS:
A.Q., G.N.R.F., L. Chambalon, 19 avril 1714; F. Genaple, 23 fév. 1693.

SUPPLIERS OF BUILDING MATERIALS:
Archives de La Charente-Maritime (La Rochelle, France), [hereafter A.C.M.] série E (minutes des notaires), J. Drouyneau, 7 fév. 1667, 22 mai 1668, 16 déc. 1669.
Archives judiciaires de Trois-Rivières [hereafter A.J.T.R.] G.N.R.F., P.F. Rigault, 26 mars 1757.
Archives nationales de France, Archives des Colonies [hereafter A.N., A.C.], série G3 (notariat de Louisbourg), carton 2041-1, 28 oct. 1751; carton 2046, 7 août 1737.
A.Q., G.N.R.F., C. Barolet, 3 oct. 1734, 27 oct. 1734 (2), 26 mars 1748, 14 nov. 1752; R. Becquet, 27 jan. 1675; L. Chambalon, 23 déc. 1692, 15 juillet 1694, 31 mai 1699(carters), 28 déc. 1701, 17 fév. 1702, 25 juin 1702, 8 nov. 1702, 21 déc. 1705, 27 mars 1706, 19 avril 1714, 17 oct. 1714, 4 juillet 1715; J.E. Dubreuil, 27 déc. 1716; F. Genaple, 13 juin 1683, 20 nov. 1692, 23 fév. 1693, 8 nov. 1695; NF 20, Prévôté de Québec, pièces detachées, 26 avril 1751.
A.Q.M., G.N.R.F., A. Adhémar, 27 déc. 1692, 6 déc. 1708 (carters); J.B. Adhémar, 14 déc. 1734, 3 jan. 1735, 13 mars 1735, 3 mai 1735 (2), 13 mai 1735; N. Gaudron de Chevremont, 3 fév. 1733; N.A. Guillet de Chaumont, 8 sept. 1732; J.C. Raimbault, 21 oct. 1729; P. Raimbault, 17 mai 1723; N. Senet, 6 mars

1727; F. Simonnet, 26 sept. 1740, 28 fév. 1743, 14 fév. 1745, 12 mars 1749, 8 sept. 1749, 22 jan. 1751, 17 jan. 1753, 24 nov. 1754, 5 nov. 1758.

CARPENTERS:

A.C.M., série E, G. Bounin, 17 août 1659; J. Drouyneau, 25 mars 1665.
A.Q., G.N.R.F., G. Audouart, 4 déc. 1650; C. Barolet, 3 avril 1748; R. Becquet, 16 oct. 1667, 28 oct. 1669; L. Chambalon, 9 oct. 1705, 2 avril 1713, 2 août 1714; J.E. Dubreuil, 18 mars 1708, 17 nov. 1719, 17 oct. 1722, 30 nov. 1722, 15 sept. 1725; P. Duquet, 27 sept. 1681, 25 fév. 1682; F. Genaple, 30 mai 1684, 10 déc. 1689; M. Piraube, 29 jan. 1640.
A.Q.M., G.N.R.F., A. Adhémar, 22 déc. 1679, 28 août 1688, 4 jan. 1689, 4 jan. 1699, 17 sept. 1700, 25 avril 1706; J.B. Adhémar, 6 oct. 1665, 12 nov. 1673, 10 déc. 1673, 19 août 1674; T. Frérot, 30 mars 1671, 27 sept. 1674; C. Maugue, 7 sept. 1680; N. Senet, 4 mai 1731; F. Simonnet, 8 avril 1747.
A.N., A.C., série G3, carton 2041-1, 30 mars 1751, 11 sept. 1752, 6 oct. 1752; carton 2042, 16 fév. 1754; carton 2044, 1 juin 1756.

JOINERS:

A.Q., G.N.R.F., J. Barbel, 2 mai 1716; C. Barolet, 29 jan. 1752, 25 avril 1752; L. Chambalon, 6 mars 1702; F. Genaple, 26 avril 1683, 24 déc. 1693, 5 fév. 1705; G. Rageot, 8 nov. 1681; J.A. Saillant, 19 août 1753.
A.Q.M., G.N.R.F., G. Barrette, 17 juin 1721, 6 mai 1736; B. Basset, 27 mai 1658, 21 sept. 1659, 22 mars 1660, 6 jan. 1669, 16 juillet 1686; P. Cabazie, 18 oct. 1689; F. Comparet, 7 avril 1739, 22 fév. 1745; N.A. Guillet de Chaumont, 19 jan. 1729, 11 sept. 1732; M. LePallieur, 21 mai 1709; J.C. Raimbault, 6 oct. 1729, 13 mars 1730.
A.J.T.R., G.N.R.F., N. Duclos, 19 fév. 1758; J. Le Proust, 14 jan. 1754, 18 mars 1757; P. Petit, 15 mars 1723; H.O. Pressé, 7 mars 1737.

MASONS:

A.C.M., série E, G. Bounin, 1er août 1660; J. Drouyneau, 25 jan. 1667, 6 juillet 1668, 27 avril 1669.
A.N., A.C., série G3, carton 2046, 13 sept. 1738.
A.Q., G.N.R.F., G. Audouart, 16 juillet 1651; C. Barolet, 9 mai 1740, 13 juillet 1749, 25 nov. 1752, 27 mai 1753, 20 mai, 1755, 3 août 1755; G. Boucault de Godefus, 16 jan. 1751; R. Becquet, 1 fév. 1679; L. Chambalon, 17 avril 1692, 3 juin 1693, 5 déc. 1697, 28 mars 1700, 18 août 1701, 17 fév. 1702, 4 mars 1702, 8 oct. 1710; J.E. Dubreuil, 24 fév. 1714, 26 juin 1719, 13 sept. 1720, 29 oct. 1720, 21 avril 1722, 29 fév. 1728, 18 oct. 1728, 28 déc. 1730; P. Duquet, 2 mars 1682, 1 fév. 1683, 11 sept. 1683; F. Genaple, 18 nov. 1682, 22 avril 1683, 13 juin 1683, 19 oct. 1683, 29 nov. 1688, 27 mai 1689, 10 déc. 1690, 3 juillet 1691, 28 sept. 1692, 4 juin 1699, 14 jan. 1700, 5 juillet 1702, 19 avril 1707; J.C. Panet, 7 sept. 1757; G. Rageot, 5 oct. 1685, 19 nov. 1689, 1er déc. 1691; S. Sanguinet, 20 juin 1755.
A.Q.M., G.N.R.F., A. Adhémar, 25 jan. 1692, 25 sept. 1692, 27 avril 1705, 17 jan. 1711; B. Basset, 30 nov. 1658, 15 fév. 1660, 11 fév. 1665, 22 fév. 1666, 4 août 1669, 22 fév. 1672; F. Comparet, 19 fév. 1741; N.A. Guillet de Chaumont, 20 déc. 1728, 21 sept. 1729, 24 jan. 1729; A. Loiseau, 30 sept. 1735; C. Maugue, 13

nov. 1695; J.C. Raimbault, 2 mars 1729, 21 sept. 1729, 20 mars 1732; P. Raimbault, 7 juillet 1726; S. Sanguinet, 30 oct. 1743.
Juridiction de Montréal, pièces détachées, 23 nov. 1660.

METALWORKERS:
A.Q., G.N.R.F., P. Lanoullier des Granges, 23 jan. 1751; J.C. Panet, 29 mai 1765 (for a mill).
A.Q.M., G.N.R.F., B. Basset, 20 mars 1660; J.C. Raimbault, 10 fév., 1731; N. Senet, 11 mai 1727.

ROOFING AND FLOORING:
A.J.T.R., G.N.R.F., P. Petit, 15 mars 1723.
A.N., A.C., série G3, carton 2046, 21 nov. 1726.
A.Q., G.N.R.F., R. Becquet, 17 fév. 1669, 3 mai 1679; L. Chambalon, 29 jan. 1696, 23 dec. 1697, 29 sept. 1701, 4 mars 1704, 11 juin 1707; J.E. Dubreuil, 4 juillet 1717; P. Duquet, 2 mars 1682; F. Genaple, 29 avril 1683, 20 déc. 1683, 9 mai 1688, 30 jan. 1696.
A.Q.M., G.N.R.F., B. Basset, 15 déc. 1659, 6 jan. 1669, 27 juin 1677; C. Maugue, 16 mars 1681; C. Moreau, 25 fév. 1686; F. Simonnet, 6 mai 1745.

Note: In addition to the above, the author consulted a smaller number of notarized experts' reports, arbitration settlements, acknowledgements of debt and workers' indentures, and these are listed in the footnotes.

Other Documentary Sources

Archives du Québec [Provincial Archives of Quebec]
   N.F. 2 Series, Ordinances of the Intendants of New France, 1666-1760.
   N.F. 11 Series, Registers of the *Conseil souverain/supérieur* at Quebec, 1663-1760.
   N.F. 13 Series, Dossiers of the *Conseil souverain/supérieur* at Quebec, 1663-1759; Vols. I, II.
   N.F. 19 Series, Registers of the *Prévôté* at Quebec, 1666-1759; Vols. VI, IX, LXXXVIII, XCV.
   N.F. 20 Series, Documents of the *Prévôté* at Quebec, 1668-1759.
   N.F. 21 Series, Documents of the Montreal jurisdiction, 1676-1760.
   N.F. 23 Series, Documents of the Trois-Rivières jurisdiction, 1646-1759; Vols. VIII, IX, XIII, XVIII.
   N.F. 25 Series, Random collection of judicial and notarial deeds, 1638-1759.
Archives privées Series, Janson-Lapalme papers.
Archives du Québec, Montreal
   Court Registers of the Montreal jurisdiction; Bailliages 1665-1682; Bailliages 1682-1687; Juridiction royale, registres des audiences, Vols. VII (1709-1713), IX (1719-1722), XI (1726-1729), XII (1730-1732), XIII (1732-1733).
   Feuillets séparés (unbound judicial documents), boxes for 1679, 1680, 1681, 1710, 1711, 1712, 1728, 1729, 1730, 1746.

Archives du Séminaire de Quebec
Manuscrits C2, C4, C5 [seminary account books, 1674-1723].
Lettres Z, No. 9.
Polygraphie Series.
Archives nationales de France, Archives des Colonies
B Series, Letters sent to the colonies in North America, 1663-1789.
C11A Series, General correspondence from Canada and dependencies, 1458-1784.
C11B Series, General correspondence from Ile-Royale and Acadia, 1712-1762.
C11D Series, General correspondence from Acadia, 1603-1788.
F3 Series, Moreau de Saint-Méry Collection on colonial administration.
La France d'Outre-mer.
G2 Series, Courts of law at Louisbourg.
G3 Series, Notarial deeds from Louisbourg and Ile-Royale.
Archives nationales de France, Archives de la Marine
A1 and A2 Series, Ordinances, edicts and decrees relating to the navy and the colonies.
Note: These documents of the Archives nationales are available on microfilm at the Public Archives of Canada, Ottawa.
Bibliothèque Saint-Sulpice (annexe), Département des documents spéciaux, Account book of the merchant Alexis Lemoyne Monière (1739-1751).
Public Archives of Canada
M.G. 1 Series, Transcripts from the Archives nationales de France, Archives des Colonies: B Series, C11A Series, F3 Series [see above].
M.G. 8 Series, Documents relating to the Province of Quebec (transcripts),
B 1, Registers of the *Prévôté* at Quebec, 1666-1759, Vols., I, II, III, IX, X, XI, XII, XX, XXXV, XXXVI.
B 3, *Prévôté de Québec*: miscellaneous documents, 1689-1746.
C 1, Court register of Montreal Island, 1644-1677.
C 5, Miscellaneous legal documents (Montreal), 1651-1700.
C 7, *Prévôté* of Cap-de-la-Madeleine, 1661-1671.
D 1, Registers from the Judicial Archives of Trois-Rivières, 1651-1689.

Unpublished Manuscripts

Fortress of Louisbourg, Preliminary Architectural Studies (1971-72):
Dunn, Brenda, "A Preliminary Study of Floors in Louisbourg" (18 pp.).
Dunn, Brenda, "A Preliminary Study of Louisbourg Ceilings" (7 pp.).
Dunn, Brenda, "Private Masonry Buildings" (80 pp.).
Hoad, Linda, "Couverture de Bardeaux" [1968] (5 pp.).
Hoad, Linda, "Doors" (18 pp.).
Hoad, Linda, "Partitions, Lambris and Panelling" (16 pp.).
Hoad, Linda, "Interior Finish" (7 pp.).
Hoad, Linda, "Windows - A Preliminary Study" (15 pp.).
Pouyez, Christian, "Rapport Préliminaire sur les Contrevents" (13 pp.).
Pouyez, Christian, "Rapport Préliminaire sur les Toits et Couvertures" (59 pp.).

Printed Works

PRIMARY WORKS

Blondel, François, *Cours d'Architecture, ou Traité de la Décoration*. 2 vols. (Paris, 1771).

Bornier, Philippe, *Conferences des Ordonnances de Louis XIV.* 2 vols (Paris, 1737).

Boucher, Pierre, *Histoire Veritable et Naturelle des Moeurs & Productions du Pays de la Nouvelle France* (Paris, 1664).

Bougainville, Louis-Antoine de (E.P. Hamilton trans.), *Adventure in the Wilderness: The American Journals of Louis-Antoine de Bougainville, 1756-1760* (Norman, 1964).

Brodeau, Julien, *Commentaire sur la Coustume de la Prevosté et Vicomté de Paris.* 2 vols. (Paris, 1658).

Bullet, Pierre, *Architecture Pratique* (Paris, 1780).

Charlevoix, Pierre François-Xavier de, *Histoire et Description Generale de la Nouvelle France.* 6 vols. (Paris, 1744).

Daviler, Charles, *Cours d'Architecture, qui comprend les Ordres de Vignole* (Paris, 1720).

Diderot, Denis and Jean-Le-Rond d'Alembert (eds.), *Encyclopedie, ou Dictionnaire raisonné des Sciences, des Arts, et des Métiers*, 17 vols. (Paris, 1751-65). *Recueil de Planches, sur les Sciences, . . . et les Arts Méchaniques.* 11 vols. (Paris, 1762-72).

Duchesne, M., *Code de la Police ou Analyse des Reglemens de Police* (Paris, 1761).

Edits, ordonnances royaux, déclarations et arrêts du Conseil d'Etat du Roi concernant le Canada. 3 vols. (Quebec, 1854-56).

Felibien, André, *Des Principes de l'Architecture, de la Sculpture, de la Peinture* (Paris, 1697).

Ferriere, Claude de, *Corps et Compilation de Tous les Commentateurs Anciens et Modernes sur la Coûtume de Paris.* 4 vols. (Paris, 1714).

Ferriere, Claude de, *Nouveau Commentaire sur la Coûtume de la Prévoté et Vicomté de Paris.* 2 vols. (Paris, 1770).

Ferriere, Claude de, *La Science Parfaite des Notaires; ou Le Parfait Notaire.* 2 vols. (Paris, 1741).

Fremin, Michel de, *Memoires Critiques d'Architecture* (Paris, 1702).

Freminville, Edmé de la Poix de, *Dictionnaire ou Traité de la Police Generale des Villes, Bourgs, Paroisses et Seigneuries de la Campagne* (Paris, 1758).

The correspondence of Governor Buade de Frontenac and the Court of France, *Rapport de l'Archiviste de la Province de Québec*, 1926-1927, 1-144; 1927- 1928, 3-211; 1928-1929, 247-384.

Furetière, Antoine, *Dictionaire Universel, Contenant generalement tous les Mots François.* 3 vols. (The Hague & Rotterdam, 1690).

Jombert, Charles A., *Architecture Moderne ou l'Art de Batir pour toutes sortes de personnes.* 2 vols. (Paris, 1728-29).

Jugements et délibérations du Conseil souverain de la Nouvelle-France (1663-1716). 6 vols. (Quebec. 1885-91.)

Kalm, Peter (J.R. Forster trans.), *Travels into North America.* 4 vols. (London, 1771).

Le Maistre, Pierre, *La Coûtume de la Prevosté et Vicomté de Paris, (Paris, 1700).*

Liger, Louis, *La Nouvelle Maison Rustique, ou Economie Generale de tous les Biens de Campagne.* 2 vols. (Paris, 1755).

Marshall, Joyce (trans. & ed.), *Word from New France: The Selected Letters of Marie de l'Incarnation* (Toronto, 1967).

Massicotte, Edouard-Zotique, *Répertoire des arrêts, édits, mandements, ordonnances et règlements conservées dans les archives du Palais de justice de Montréal, 1640-1760,* (Montreal, 1919).

Perrault, Joseph-François, *Extraits ou Précédens, tirés des registres de la Prevosté de Québec,* [1726-1756] (Quebec, 1824).

Pichon, Thomas, *Lettres et Memoires Pour Servir a l'Histoire Naturelle,* Civile et *Politique du Cap Breton* (The Hague, 1760).

Roy, Antoine (ed.), *L'Ile de Montréal en 1731* (Quebec, 1943).

Roy, Pierre-Georges, *Inventaire des ordonnances des Intendants de la Nouvelle-France.* 4 vols. (Beauceville, 1919).

Roy, Pierre-Georges (ed.), *Ordonnances, commissions, etc., etc., des Gouverneurs et Intendants de la Nouvelle-France, 1639-1706. 2 vols.* (Beauceville, 1924).

De la Rue, J.B., *Traité de la Coupe des Pierres* (Paris, 1728).

Savot, Louis (F. Blondel ed.), *L'Architecture Françoise des Bastimens Particuliers* (Paris, 1685).

Stone, W.L. (ed.), *Letters of Brunswick and Hessian Officers during the American Revolution* (Albany, 1891).

Thwaites, Reuben Gold (ed.), *The Jesuit Relations and Allied Documents: Travels and explorations of the Jesuit missionaries in New France 1610-1791.* 73 vols. (Cleveland, 1896-1901).

Vignola, Giacoma (Pierre Esquié ed., W.R. Powell trans.), *Vignola, an Elementary Treatise on Architecture* (Cleveland, 1922).

Wrong, George M. (ed.), *Lettre d'un Habitant de Louisbourg, 1745* (Toronto, 1896).

SECONDARY WORKS

Auger, Roland-J., *La Grande Recrue de 1653* (Montreal, 1955).

Babelon, Jean-Pierre, *Demeures parisiennes sous Henri IV et Louis XIII,* (Paris, 1965).

Chambaud, Louis, *Dictionnaire François-Anglois & Anglois-François.* 2 vols. (London, 1815).

Cotgrave, Randle, *A Dictionarie of the French and English Tongues* (London, 1611).

Cox, Richard E., "Wooden Shingles from the Fortress of Louisbourg," *Bulletin of the Association for Preservation Technology* [hereafter B.A.P.T.], Vol.II (1970), Nos. 1-2, 65-69.

Doyon, Georges & Robert Hubrecht, *L'Architecture rurale & bourgeoise en France,* (Paris, 1957).

Gauthier-Larouche, Georges, *Evolution de la Maison rurale traditionnelle dans la région de Québec* (Quebec, 1974).

Hoad, Linda, "Wood Shingles in 18th Century Louisbourg," *B.A.P.T.,* Vol.II (1970), Nos.1-2, 62-65.

Jury, Wilfrid and Elsie McLeod Jury, *Sainte-Marie Among the Hurons* (Toronto, 1954).

135

Kidd, Kenneth E., *The Excavation of Sainte-Marie I* (Toronto, 1949).

Krause, Eric R., "Private Buildings in Louisbourg, 1713-1758," *Canada, an Historical Magazine*, Vol.I, No.4 (June, 1974), 47-59.

Laframboise, Yves, *L'Architecture traditionnelle au Québec* (Montreal, 1975).

Lessard, Michel & Gilles Vilandré, *La Maison traditionnelle au Québec* (Montreal, 1974).

Massicotte, Edouard-Zotique, "L'Incendie du Vieux Montréal," *Bulletin des Recherches historiques* [hereafter B.R.H.], Vol.XXXII (1926), 583-608. "Maçons, entrepreneurs, architectes," *B.R.H.*, Vol.XXXV (1929), 132-142.

Morisset, Gérard, *L'Architecture en Nouvelle-France* (Quebec, 1949).

Nute, Grace Lee, *The Voyageur* (St. Paul, 1955).

Rempel, John I., *Building in Wood* (Toronto, 1967).

Richardson, A.J.H., "A Comparative Historical Study of Timber Building in Canada," *B.A.P.T.*, Vol.V (1973), No. 3, 77-100. "Early Roofing Materials," *B.A.P.T.*, Vol.II (1970). Nos.1-2, 18-27. "Guide to the architecturally and historically most significant Buildings in the Old City of Quebec," *B.A.P.T.*, Vol.II (1970), Nos.3-4, entire issue.

Ritchie, Thomas, *Canada Builds, 1867-1967* (Ottawa, 1967).

Roy, Antoine, *Les Lettres, les sciences et les arts au Canada sous le régime français (Paris, 1930).*

Séguin, Robert-Lionel, *La Maison en Nouvelle-France* (Ottawa, 1968) [This booklet published by the National Museum of Canada reproduces many extracts from the notarial files of Antoine Adhémar and other Montreal notaries.]. *Les Granges au Québec* (Ottawa, 1963).

Shurtleff, Harold R., *The Log Cabin Myth* (Cambridge Mass., 1939).

Sloane, Eric, *A Museum of Early American Tools* (New York, 1973). *A Reverence for Wood* (New York, 1973).

Tanguay, Cyprien, *Dictionnaire généalogique des familles canadiennes depuis la fondation de la colonie jusqu'à nos jours.* 7 vols. (Montreal, 1871-90).

Traquair, Ramsay, *The Old Architecture of Quebec* (Toronto, 1947).

Trudel, Marcel (ed.), *Atlas de la Nouvelle-France/An Atlas of New France* (Quebec, 1968). *Introduction to New France* (Toronto, 1968).

Credits

Page 2: Musée Carnavalet, Cris de Paris, 3rd series (1737-38).

Page 19: From Ramsy Traquair, *The Old Architecture of Quebec*. Toronto: Macmillan, 1947, p. 284.

Page 23: From Alan Gowans, *Building Canada*.. Toronto: Oxford, 1966, plate 11; and Thomas Ritchie, *Canada Builds*. National Research Council. Toronto: University of Toronto Press, 1967, p. 62.

Page 24: From a slide by Peter N. Moogk.

Page 25: From M. Lessard and G. Vilandré, *La Maison Traditionnelle au Québec*. Montreal: Les Editions de l'homme Ltée., 1972, p. 111.

Page 26: Archives nationales de France, Archives d'outre-mer, G2 Series, Vol. 201, dossier 250.

Page 28: Lessard and Villandré, p. 111.

Page 29: From Robert-Louis Séguin, *La Maison en Nouvelle-France,* National Museum of Canada, Bulletin 226, Ottawa, 1968, p. 35, and a photograph by Peter N. Moogk.

Page 31, Top: From a slide by Peter N. Moogk.

Page 31, Bottom: From a slide by Peter N. Moogk.

Page 33: From André Félibien, *Des Principes de l'Architecture*. Paris: La Veuve & Jean Baptiste Coignard, 1967.

Page 36: From Yves Laframboise, *L'Architecture traditionnelle au Québec*. Montreal: Les Editions de l'homme Ltée., p. 181.

Page 38: Traquair, p. 41.

Page 42: From *Association for Preservation of Technology Bulletin*, Vol. 11 (Nos. 3-4), 1970, p. 104.

Page 44; Traquair, p. 47.

Page 45: Lessard and Villandré, p. 145.

Page 51: University of Toronto, Fine Arts Department, Slide Collection.

Page 52: Lessard and Villandré, p. 248.

Page 53: From a slide by Peter N. Moogk.

Pages 54-55: From Michel Lessard and Hughette Marquis, *Encyclopédie de la Maison Québécoise*. Montreal: Les Editions de l'homme Ltée., 1972, p. 513, and slides and photographs by Peter N. Moogk.

Page 58: A.N.Q., G.N.R.F., Romain Bequet, 3 mai 1679, p. 1.

Page 65, Top: National Map Collection, Public Archives of Canada. From "Carte du Fort St. Louis de Quebec par Jean Baptiste Louis Franquelin, 1683." Archives nationales, Paris, Dépôt des Fortifications des Colonies, Carton 6, Pièce No. 347.

Page 65, Bottom: National Map Collection, Public Archives of Canada. From "Anonymous," D.F.C. 375.A. Bibliothèque Nationale de France.

Page 66: National Map Collection, Public Archives of Canada. From "Plan de la ville de Montréal dans la Nouvelle France, 1731." By Chaussegros de Léry, Gaspard-Joseph, 1682-1756. British Museum, London, Add. Mss. 15331, no. 28.

Page 67: Photograph by Peter N. Moogk.

Page 68, Top: courtesy Fortress Louisbourg.

Page 68, Bottom: Parks Canada Photograph.

Page 69: From Denis Diderot and Jean-Le-Rond d'Alembert, eds., *Recueil de Planches, sur les Sciences, . . . et les Arts Méchaniques.* 11 vols., Paris: Le Breton; 1762-72, II, *Charpente,* plate I.

Page 70: J.B. de la Rue, *Traité de la Coupe des Pierres.* Paris: 1728, Frontispiece. Publication date is 1728 despite "1738" in engraving.

Page 71: Archives nationales de France, Archives des Colonies, série C11A, Vol. 126, "Profil et Elevation du Logement du Commendent [sic] du Port Toulouze" and "Plan du Logement" by Etienne Verrier, 1733.

Page 72, Top: The National Gallery of Canada, Ottawa.

Page 72, Bottom: The National Gallery of Canada, Ottawa.

Page 75: Author's conception.

Page 76, Top: Archives nationales du Québec (Montréal), Greffes des Notaires du régime français, Bénigne Basset, 22 fev. 1672, No. 728, masonry contract between Milot, de Vennes, and Bouvier, p. 11, top half.

Page 76, Bottom: Author's conception.

Page 78: Plan appended to building contract drawn up Dec.20, 1728, by the notary Guillet de Chaumont.

Page 79: Projection of the specifications given in the Dec. 20, 1728, building contract drawn up by the notary, Guillet de Chaumont.

Page 81: Laframboise, p. 250 and a slide by Peter N. Moogk.

Page 83: Traquair, p. 44.

Page 84, Top Left: Laframboise, p. 235.

Page 84, Top Right: Traquair, p. 283.

Page 84, Middle: Sainte-Marie among the Hurons.

Page 84, Bottom: *Ibid.*

Page 96: Archives nationales du Québec, Greffes des Notaires du régime français, Romain Becquet, ler fev., 1679, p. 1.

Page 97: Félibien.

Page 98: *Ibid.*

Page 99: *Ibid.*

Page 102: Leonodiff *et al., Comment Restaurer une Maison traditionnelle.* Quebec: Ministère des Affaires Culturelles, 1973, p. 34.

Page 105: Félibien.

Page 106, Left: Traquair, p. 286.

Page 106, Right: Laframboise, p. 236.

Page 120: From a slide by Peter N. Moogk.

Page 121: From J.R. Harper, *Painting in Canada.* Toronto: University of Toronto Press, 1966, p. 123.

Index

A

Acadia: 14, 29, 31, 46n, 67, 71, 119
Accoyau (corbel): 60, 123
A queue d'aronde (dovetailing): 30,
31, 78, 112
Attic: 27, 57, 80, 82, 104

B

Bake oven: 37, 76, 90, 117
Bolts: 37, 83, 84, 85, 106, 107, 125;
draw, 106; sliding, 83, 84, 85, 107,
125; spring, 85
Brick: 24, 53, 57, 77, 90, 95; for
chimney flues, 53; as fill, 24; as
fireproofing, 57; at Louisbourg, 90

C

Cave (cellar): 27, 37, 40, 57, 60, 61,
77, 81, 85, 104, 106, 123
Ceiling: 27, 35, 37, 42, 104, 106
Chimney: 18, 27, 36, 37-38, 51, 52-56,
57, 59, 60, 80, 90, 111, 117, 119,
124; building regulations, 50-56;
cleaning of, 52; contracts for, 53, 59;
dimensions of, 52; as a fire hazard,
51, 52-54; flues, 18, 52, 53-54, 90,
124; and gables, 18; *languettes,* 18,
124; liability for, 111; location of,
37; masonry, 36; in Montreal, 52-
56; in Quebec, 52-54, 56, 60; and
shingles, 56; stone, 51, 52; sweeps,
52-53; wattleand daub, 36
Colombage (see also half-timbering):
8, 24, 25, 26, 27, 28, 32, 35, 37, 40,
42, 49, 56, 57, 67, 69, 94, 119, 123;
colombage bousillé, 24; *colombage
pierroté,* 24, 27; *en colombage,* 28;
maison en colombage, 24, 28, 56
Contracts (see also *legal
considerations*): 9, 11, 12, 25, 27, 31,
34, 35-37, 38-39, 40-41, 47n, 49, 53,
59, 60, 61-62, 73, 74, 77, 78-79, 80-
81, 82-83, 85-86, 89-90, 91, 92, 95,
100-01, 103, 104, 106, 110-17, 119,
123, 124, 126-30; agricultural
considerations, 34, 62; *à la toise,* 59-
60, 61, 80, 110; arbitration of, 113,
114; armed protection, 35; bonuses,
39; Bourdon/Grouvel, 25, 27;
builder's liability, 110-11;
carpentry, 61; chimneys, 53, 59;
regarding *colombage* construction,
27; court cases involving, 39, 85-86;
Crown, 83, 89; deception in, 116;
delays, 100-01; *devis,* 89-90, 107,
124; economic considerations, 34,
35, 36, 59, 61; *eau-de-vie,* 39; *en
bloc,* 59, 61, 124; farmhouses, 25,
27, 35, 36, 37, 38-39, 41; floors, 59;
A. Forestier contract, 80-81, 82-83,
85; J.-B. Forestier contract, 73, 74,
77, 78-79, 126-30; foundations, 40;
au fur et à mesure, 40, 115, 123;
inspection, 110, 113; interpretation,
115; ignorance of, 116; Lajoue stone
contract, 92; Le Beau contract, 112-
13; *marché les clefs à la main,* 59,
61, 114, 124; masonry, 49, 59, 60,
61, 83; non-fulfilment, 111-12, 113;
notarized, 106, 115; partial
payments, 40-41; payment of, 36-
37, 39, 40, 59, 110, 114, 115, 123;
regarding *pièces-sur-pièces*
construction, 31; roof, 59, 101, 103,
104; sealing of, 38-39; seasonal
considerations, 38, 39, 41, 61-62; for
stone buildings, 60, 61, 91;
subcontractors, 59, 61, 77, 114;
verbal agreement, 114; Verrier/
Richomme, 37; Vinét/Trudeau, 35-
37; warranty, 111
Couverture chevauchée (lapped board
roof): 28, 36, 42, 56-57, 72, 103,
113
Crépi or *gobetage* (roughcast wall
covering): 44, 45, 80, 95, 124
Croix de Sainte-André (diagonal and
intersecting braces): 42, 124

D

Devis des ouvrages (statement of work
to be done): 89-90, 107, 124

Door: 37, 38, 40, 41, 42, 62, 72, 78,
82, 85, 91, 92, 95, 104, 106, 107,
124; *brisés a panneaux couverts,* 78;
construction of, 40; hardware, 85,
106, 107; latch, 85, 106, 107, 124;
locks, 82, 85, 106; number of, 38
Dovetailing: 30, 31, 78, 112

E

Eaves: 22, 36, 42, 45, 101
Excavation of foundations: 81, 82

F

Facade: 27, 28, 95; masonry, 27;
stone, 28, 95
Farmhouse: 22-45, 72, 101, 120; barn,
27, 30, 37; *bousillage,* 36; brick, 24;
cellar, 40; clay fill, 45; *colombage,*
32, 35, 37, 40, 42; contracts for, 25,
27, 35, 36, 37, 38-39, 41; *Croix de
Sainte-André,* 42; dovetailing, 30-
31; exterior walls, 43-44, 45; frame,
37, 40, 41-42; half-timbering, 24,
25, 26, 27-28; interior partitions, 42-
43; masonry, 28, 44; *pièces-sur-
pièces* construction, 29, 30, 31-32,
34-35, 37, 44, 45, 120; *piquets,* 29;
pieux, 31; *planches chevauchées,* 36,
42; Red River Frame, 32; relation to
France, 22, 23; roof of, 22-23, 42,
45; Ross house, 32; Sherman Hall
observations, 39-40; sills, 40, 41;
sollivaux passans, 35; stone and
mortar fill, 25, 45; timber of, 23-24,
28, 39, 45; Villeneuve house, 23;
Vinet house, 35, 36; walls, 30-31
Fiche (hinge): 85, 106, 124
Filières (purlin): 57, 124
Fill: 24, 25, 27, 28, 29, 32, 34, 41, 44,
45, 77, 119; bonding of, 28; brick,
24; clay, 45; clay and straw, 28;
fibre and clay, 44; masonry, 28, 77;
plaster and rubble, 27, 28, 119;
roughcasting, 29; stone and mortar,
24, 25, 28, 45; stone and mud or
clay, 24; wood, 28, 29, 34
Fireplace: 18, 27, 35, 53, 80, 81, 85,
92, 106; hardware, 85; and hearth,
18; and mantle, 35; stone, 80, 81
Fire prevention: 50-56, 119
Floor: 31, 35, 36, 37, 39, 42, 57, 59,

60, 62, 74-75, 78, 82, 94, 104, 106,
112; *à jointes carrées,* 106; *cannelé,*
74; cedar or pine boards butted, 36,
74; contracts for, 59; decay in, 60;
earthen, 31; insulation, 74; plan, 74-
75, 78; planks, 106; seasoned
boards, 39; tongue and groove, 112
Flues: 18, 52, 53-54, 90, 124
Forestier, A., house: 80-83, 85-86;
attic, 80-82; cellar, 81; chimneys, 80,
81; clean up, 82; contracts for, 80-
81, 82-83, 85; cost, 80-81, 82, 85;
dimensions, 81, 82; doors, 82;
dressed stone, 80; floors, 82;
foundation 81, 82; frame, 82;
gables, 80; hardware, 85; hearths,
81; ironwork, 85; joints, 80; locks,
85; *marché à la toise,* 81; masonry,
80, 82; mortar, 80; nails, 83; outside
walls, 80; payment, 82; planks, 82-
83; plans, 80-81; plaster, 80; roof
frame, 82; roughcasting, 80;
shutters, 82; whitewash, 80;
windows, 82
Forestier, J.-B., house: 73-75, 77-80,
126-30; beams, 77; bricks, 77;
cannelé, 74; caulking, 74; cellar, 77;
clearing building site, 77; contract,
73, 74, 77, 78-79; cupboards, 75, 78;
doors, 78; dovetailing, 78; dressed
stone, 77; economy, 77; floor plan,
74-75, 78; floor materials, 74-75;
foundation, 77; gabled wall, 80;
hearth, 74, 75, 77; hinges, 78; inside
walls, 77; ironwork, 77; masonry,
77, 78; masonry fill, 77; outside
walls, 77; partition walls, 75, 77, 78;
payment, 79; plaster, 80; price, 74,
77-78; roof, 78, 79; roughcasting,
77, 80; salvage, 77; sink, 75, 80;
stairway, 78; stone gables, 79;
tambour, 75; whitewash, 80;
windows, 78, 79
Foundation: 23, 27, 36, 40, 41, 62, 77,
81, 82, 91, 94; *colombage,* 40;
contracts for, 40; dimensions, 40,
94; stone, 27, 36, 40; stone and
mortar, 40
Frames: 8, 24, 27, 28, 30, 32, 34, 35,
37, 38, 39, 40, 41-42, 44, 45, 57, 59,
72, 80, 82, 91, 103-04, 112, 119;

ash, 38; butternut, 37, 38; cedar, 27, 38; cost, 59; dressing, 35; durability, 32; fire hazards, 57; hemlock, 37, 38; oak, 37, 38; raising of, 41; roof, 37, 40, 42, 56, 62, 69, 82, 89, 101, 103-04, 120; securing of, 30; stone, 24, 45, 57, 72, 80; window, 91, 112; wooden, 24, 28, 32, 37, 38, 39, 40, 44, 45, 57

G

Gables: 18, 26, 27, 35, 42, 52, 54-55, 57, 60, 62, 80, 101, 104, 110, 119, 121; *colombage*, 26, 27, 35; common, 18; as fire protection, 52, 54-55, 57, 60, 101, 119, 121; masonry, 62; stone, 57, 60; wall, 80, 110

Gambrel or mansard: 27, 28

Gond (iron pintle): 85, 124

Grand Voyer (Overseer of Highways): 16, 17

H

Half-timbering (see also *colombage*): 24, 25, 26, 27-28, 32, 35, 37, 40, 42, 67, 69, 119

Hazards: 16-17, 50-56, 60, 72, 95; decay, 60; falling stone, 95; fire, 50-56; shingles, 56; workmen's injuries, 95

Hearth: 18, 57, 74, 77, 80, 81, 106

Hinge: 37, 78, 85, 106, 107, 124; iron, 37; strap, 106, 107

Holograph contracts: 78-79

House alignments: 16-17, 18, 57

I

Insulation: 28, 32

Ironwork: 37, 51, 59, 77, 85, 106, 107, 116

J

Joiners: 11, 18, 50, 77, 82, 101, 104, 106, 111, 112, 113

L

Labourers: 11, 18, 26, 27, 28, 31, 33, 34, 35, 37, 39, 40-41, 42, 50, 61, 62-63, 77, 82, 88, 93, 94, 99, 100-01, 104, 110-11, 114-15, 116; accounts, 99; absenteeism, 100-01; delays, 100; fines, 100; wages, 100, 116

Lait de chaux (whitewash): 44, 124

Lambourdes (joists): 83, 124

Languettes (chimney flue dividers): 18, 124

Latch: 85, 106, 107, 124

Legal considerations (see also *contracts*): 12, 13-20, 25, 27, 50-57, 59-60, 95, 100-01, 103, 110-17; chimneys, 52-56; creditors, 17; delays and absenteeism, 100-01; Dupuy building ordinance, 57, 59-60, 103; English Common Law, 17; falling stone, 95; fire prevention, 50-56, 57; French civil law, 17, 18; latrines, 50; liability, 110-17; return of money, 60; street allowances, 14, 16, 50; title, 17

Locks: 82, 85, 106

Loquet à boucle (ring-latch): 85

Loquet à poignée (thumb latch): 85, 124

Louisbourg: 14-15, 16, 17, 24, 26, 27, 37, 47n, 49, 53-54, 63n, 67, 88, 90, 101, 103, 109n, 111, 119, 120-21; brick used in, 90; *colombage* construction, 27; chimney regulations, 53-54; delays, 101; and the fishery, 24; and France, 24; hospital and quayside quarter, 67; merchant builders, 88, 90; map of, 66; Presqu'Ile du Quay, 15; size of lots, 15, 16, 17; use of shingles, 103, 109n; timber housing in, 24, 29, 120

M

Madriers (heavy planks): 82, 83, 124

Maison en colombage: 24, 28

Mansard roof: 57, 58, 60

Masonry, Masons: 11, 12, 17, 27-28, 36, 44, 49, 50-52, 57, 59, 60, 61, 62, 67, 72, 77, 78, 80, 81, 82, 88, 89, 92, 94, 95, 99, 110, 115, 116, 117, 120; *à la toise,* 59-60, 110; in attics, 57; clientele using, 60, 61; climate considerations, 61-62; contractors, 88, 89, 102; contracts for, 49, 59, 60, 61; cost of, 60; exteriors, 44, 49, 50-52, 60; fill, 28, 77; final inspection, 110; in fireplaces, 80; and mortar,

61, 80, 90; partnerships in, 59; with roughcasting, 72, 110; rubble stone, 59; tools used in, 94, 95, 96, 97-98; in walls, 62

Metalworkers: 11, 106

Montreal: see *Ville Marie de Montréal*

Mortar: 61, 80, 90, 91, 92, 94, 95, 103, 116, 117

Mortise and Tenon Joints: 30, 32, 40, 41

Mur mitoyen (common wall): 17-18, 19, 124

N

Nails: 42, 79, 83, 103, 112

Notary: 11, 35, 38, 51, 61, 74, 75

O

Oven: 37, 76, 90, 117

P

Partition walls: 27, 43, 104, 112

Patte (iron pin): 85, 124

Penture (strap hinge): 85, 124

Pièces-sur-pièces: 28-30, 31-32, 34-35, 37, 38, 44-45, 46, 48n, 49, 57, 59, 60, 119, 120; contracts for, 31; cost, 34, 59; durability, 32, 34; *en pièces-sur-pièces,* 119; as insulation, 32; *pièces de bois sur pièces de bois,* 28

Pierre de grès (sandstone): 90, 125

Piquets (round posts): 29, 31, 67, 80, 120, 125; *en piquets,* 120

Planche (thin board): 83, 125

Planches chevauchées (overlapping boards): 28, 36, 42, 56-57, 72, 103

Plankwall construction: 23, 48n

Pot-de-vin (gratuity): 39, 125

Prévôté: 17, 18, 50, 56, 107, 113, 115, 117, 125

Pruche (hemlock tree): 38, 47n, 125

Purlin: 57, 124

Q

Quebec City: 13, 14, 15, 16-17, 18, 22, 24, 25, 27-28, 31, 39, 45, 49, 50, 51-54, 56-57, 60, 61-62, 63n, 65, 76, 77, 80, 86, 89, 90, 91, 92-93, 94-95, 99-101, 103-04, 106-07, 110, 111, 115, 119, 120; chimney regulations, 52-54, 56, 60; climate, 61-62;

colombage construction in, 49; *colombage pierroté* construction in, 24, 27; Côte de la Montagne Road, 51; crusade against wooden structures, 56-57; fires, 50, 51-52, 60; imaginary construction site, 93, 94-95, 99-101, 103-04, 106-07; latrines in, 50; Lower Town, 14, 15, 50, 51-52, 56, 91, 102; masonry construction in, 120; merchant builders, 90-91, 99-101; map of, 65; mansard roofs in, 57; *pièces-sur-pièces* construction in, 49; *pieux* construction in, 31; Place Royale, 14; population of, 49; public hazards, 16-17, 50, 51-52; roofs in, 101; Saint-Jean Street, 14; Saint-Louis Street, 14; Sainte-Pierre Street, 91; sand gathering, 92-93; shingles used in, 56, 103; speculation, 15; stone construction in, 27-28, 60, 90-91; Upper Town, 14, 51-52, 94; as a village, 27

R

Raising a house frame: 40-42

Roof: 8, 22-23, 25, 26, 27, 28, 35, 36, 37, 40, 41-42, 45, 50, 52, 56, 57, 59, 60, 62, 69, 71, 72, 78, 79, 82, 90, 101, 103-04, 105, 109n, 110, 113-14, 120, 123, 124; bellcast, 119; board, 11, 23, 25, 56, 71, 72, 90, 101, 103, 113; and chimneys, 52; climate considerations, 62, 103, 104; contracts, 59, 101, 103, 104; corbels, 123; *couverture chevauchée, Croix de Sainte-André* bracing, 42, 124; farmhouse, 22-23, 42, 45; *faux entrait,* 101; and fires, 57; frame, 37, 40, 42, 56, 62, 69, 82, 89, 101, 103-04, 105, 110, 113-14, 120, 123, 124; gambrel or mansard, 26, 27; use of lime, 103; low-pitched, 45; mansard, 57, 58, 60; oblong, hipped, 22; pine board, 28, 103; of *planches chevauchées,* 36, 42; on purlins, 57; in Quebec City, 101; Louis Savot observations, 22-23; shakes, 28; shingles, 23, 42, 56, 57, 72, 79, 101, 103-04; slate, 56, 57, 103; slope and height, 23; stone,

119; straw covering, 45; thatch, 72; tile, 22, 56, 57, 103; tin leaf, 56; tongue and groove, 42, 103, 113; tools used in construction, 105; trusses, 41-42, 57; on Villeneuve house, 23
Rooms: 42-43, 75, 78
Roughcasting: 29, 45, 72, 77, 80, 92, 95, 103, 110

S
Salvage: 37, 77, 85, 86n, 91
Sand: 92-93, 94
Shingles: 23, 42, 50, 56, 57, 72, 79, 101, 103-04, 109n; cedar, 57, 101, 103-04; dimensions, 101, 103; as a fire hazard, 56, 57; payment for, 103; pine, 103
Shutters: 37, 38, 72, 82, 83, 85, 104, 107; hardware for, 85, 107
Sill (sole): 24, 37, 38, 40, 41, 83, 104, 125
Stone: 23, 24, 25, 27-28, 36, 40, 44, 45, 49, 51, 52, 53, 56, 57, 59, 60, 61, 72, 77, 80, 90-91, 92, 94, 95, 107, 111, 114, 116, 117, 120-21, 123, 125; availability of, 28; Beauport stone, 91; brick, 24, 53, 57, 77, 90, 95; Le Cap stone, 91; in chimneys, 51, 52; clientele for, 60; climate considerations, 61-62; corbels, 60, 123; cost, 59, 61, 91; cutting and dressing, 61, 77, 80, 91-92; dimensions of dwellings, 61; fieldstone, 91; in fireplaces, 80, 81; in foundations, 27, 36, 40; as frame for openings, 24, 45, 57, 72, 80; in gables, 57, 79; in hearths, 80; limestone, 90, 91, 125; payment for, 92; Pointe-aux-Trembles greystone, 91; prefabrication, 91; in Quebec construction, 27-28, 60, 90-91; in roofs, 119; samples, 92; sandstone, 90; seasonal considerations, 91-92; supply of, 59; as walls, 23, 24, 25, 44, 45, 49, 95; windows, 114
Street allowances: 14, 16, 50
Stonemasons: 59, 70, 91-92, 94-98
Subcontractors: 59, 61, 77, 114

T
Tambour (covered vestibule): 75, 125

Targette (sliding bolt): 85, 107, 125
Targettes à ressort (spring-bolts): 85
Trois-Rivières: 14, 27, 49, 50, 60, 63n, 88, 111, 113, 114; colombage construction in, 27; crusade against wooden buildings, 60; fires, 50; merchant builders, 88; methods of construction, 49

V
Ville Marie de Montréal: 13, 14, 15, 16, 19, 22, 27, 28, 31, 34, 35, 49, 50, 52-56, 60, 62, 63n, 64n, 66, 73, 75, 77, 80, 85, 86, 88, 89, 92, 93, 94, 95, 100, 103, 104, 106, 108n, 111, 112-13, 114, 117; Château de Ramezay, 73, 92; chimney regulations, 52-56; colombage construction in, 27; Corpus Christi fire, 56, 64n; crusade against wooden structures, 56-57, 60; defence of, 15; fire, 50, 52, 56, 57; Hôtel-Dieu, 19, 56, 99; maison en colombage construction in, 28, 56; map of, 66; masonry construction in, 49; merchant builders, 88, 89, 95; pièces-sur-pièces construction in, 49; pieux construction in, 31; public thoroughfares, 16; seventeenth century wood construction, 34; size of lots, 15; solid wooden houses in, 28, 49; stone construction in, 49, 57
Vin de marché: 39, 125
Verrou (cross-bolt): 85, 125

W
Walls: 17-18, 19, 23, 24, 25, 27, 28, 30-31, 32, 35, 42-44, 45, 46, 60, 61, 62, 92, 94, 95, 103, 104, 112; bays, 30; bousillage, 36, 123; climate considerations, 62; construction methods, 94, 95; contre-murs, 19, 124; crépi, 44, 45, 80, 95, 124; dimensions, 94; exterior, 27, 35, 43-44, 45, 77, 80, 95; enduit, 80, 124; fill, 24, 25; and gables, 27, 80; interior, 27, 42-43, 75, 77, 78, 112; knee, 27; masonry, 62; mur mitoyen, 17-18, 19, 124; parapet, 60; plate, 24, 27, 41, 103; protective boarding, 19, 25; rubble, 61, 72; stone, 23, 24,

25, 44, 45, 49, 92, 94-95; wall
boards, 25; weather boarding, 25;
wood, 23, 27, 28, 32, 71, 72
Windows: 19, 37, 38, 40, 41, 42, 45,
47n, 62, 72, 77-78, 82, 83, 84, 85,
91, 92, 95, 104, 106, 107, 109n, 112,
114; barring, 19; casement, 37, 38,
83, 104, 107, 109n; construction of,
40; frames, 91, 112; glass, 38, 45;
hardware, 83, 85, 107; hinges, 107;
number of, 38; oiled paper, 38, 45,
47n; *panneau,* 85; shutters, 37, 38,
72, 82, 83, 85, 104, 107; sills, 37, 38,
40, 41, 104; stone, 114